ADVENTURES IN FRANCE

JOANNE HOMER

Copyright © 2020 Joanne Homer

The right of Joanne Homer to be identified as the Author of the Work has been asserted in accordance with The Copyright, Design and Patents Act 1988

Visit my website and subscribe for your free

EBook

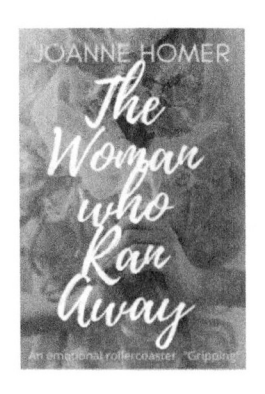

www.joannehomer.com

Face book – joannehomerauthor

Instagram – joanne.homerbooks

Chapter 1

I don't quite recall where the idea came from to live in France, but it happened somewhere along the way, probably due to a severe of lack of money. But it was a dream I had and it kept me going. There are properties to be bought in France for next to nothing, but it has to be said, that you would need to spend a significant sum of money on them. I also happen to admire the French immensely.

But I have patience, I have practical knowledge and I have time on my hands, however, money is sadly lacking. And then one day I had a fantasy. As I was looking on the internet for properties in France, I discovered something. In France you can buy a Chateau for the price of a three bedroom detached house in the part of the world where I live. If you lived in London it would be the price of a shabby three bedroom ex-council house.

And then up she popped. That red-haired, buxom vixen had stolen my dream. Not only was she about to buy a Chateau, she was also married to some ageing bloke who would make it happen. To say I was pig sick is an understatement. But everyone loved the TV series, and ashamed as I am to say it, I watched it too.

I cannot hear their names without going pff, pff, pff, in a mock spitting action, because I am green with envy. Their 'house' (nay Chateau) is the stuff of dreams. Pepper pot turrets moat complete with stables, walled vegetable garden and 'Orangery' is the stuff of my fantasies. How dare they steal my dream?

But they have the money and I don't.

That makes it worse.

I am old, far too old to do that now, but I still have a dream; a dream of living in a little stone house somewhere in rural France. Being able to make a meagre living from my novels and living off the land. But it is still a dream and I am 54, not like the scarlet-haired vixen who is much younger.

Oh well, some things are not to be, but still I persevere.

There is an upside to all of this. There is a little hovel in France that I adore with a passion, but it doesn't belong to me, it belongs to my former partner and he is totally disillusioned with it. It is in a little commune in Brittany. Not as grand as the Pays de Loire I grant you, but nevertheless it is beautiful there.

But I digress. I will go back to the beginning.

I met 'A' (as I will call him) in the year 2010. We had known each other many years before and I won't bore you with the details as you can read them in my novel based on a true story; "The Woman who Ran Way" if you so wish, but it is not necessary.

Now while we were together, we had no money, but he had a dream (as they say) and that dream was living in France. It was cheap there and once that seed of an idea had been planted in my mind it grew like Topsy. My only taste of France had been a trip to Paris, and I loved it. I still do. In my fantasies I am half French. My personality, my passion, my drama, and my ice queen persona are all down to the fact that I am (at least in my dreams) half French. I blame my brother who once did one of those cheap genealogies and announced with a flourish that our surname was not some common West Midlands name, but we were actually descendants from some Norman French nobility.

How proud I was. Even if I doubted the authenticity of such a genealogy, I believed in it all the same.

Back to the hovel; well it is not a hovel, well yes it is. I will explain.

'A' was working in Saudi, and earning handsome money; so much so, that within the space of 18 months he had amassed a whopping £35,000 and he was looking to buy a house.

Despite his first thoughts of France, he started to look in Ireland, and even went there on a trip to view properties whilst on leave from Saudi. But the Irish are what they are, and after many a false start he abandoned the idea after spending considerable money on a trip to Ireland. He had placed a deposit on a property, only to find that the land was being sold under false pretences. He did eventually get his money back, but not without some threats being issued. I am sure this isn't typical of the Irish, but he had a bad time, as he always does, it would seem.

He then turned his attention back to France, much to my relief. Now at that time we weren't having a relationship and we were just 'good friends' although I did have his three year old child, Clara. We emailed regularly and he Skyped his daughter once a week although she was young and had the attention span of a gnat.

In his moments of leisure when he was not working, he browsed the internet and sent me properties in France that he liked.

I have to say that they were pitiful. They needed too much doing to them, or they were too close to other properties. None of them had any land, which was a pre-requisite if you wanted to grow veg and keep animals (which would fit in with his dream of self sufficiency).

And then he sent me a picture of one together with the details. I thought 'this has potential'.

It had nearly six acres of land, some of which adjoined the property (which is rare in France). The roof had been replaced recently, and the place had been gutted. What was most exciting about it, was that it had three 'ruins' adjacent, that were made of stone. It was also very close to the Nantes Breste Canal. In short, it was picture postcard perfect.

When I expressed excitement about this property, 'A' was having none of it. He suggested that there was too much land. I proffered the opinion that it was just enough and that he could always let it out for grazing if needs be. But it lay there on the back burner, so to speak and was not spoken of again. I knew when not to push things with 'A'.

Chapter 2

It was three months later, when 'A' told me he was coming back to Britain, and had planned a trip to France to look at properties. He asked if I would go with him. I had my misgivings about going. Least of all, because I was still madly in love with him, and thought he was no longer in love with me. I took some persuading to say yes to the trip, but eventually I succumbed, largely out of pity.

He had booked the ferry for late April, and he had booked the trains to get to Portsmouth. He had arranged for a hire car in France, and accommodation in a Romany caravan for the duration. If nothing else, it would be a mini break, so I thought.

I collected him from Heathrow airport, as he had asked me to, and he paid for my petrol. The next day we went shopping for clothes. He was in good humour and seemed excited about the trip, as was I.

The ferry was fantastic. I have travelled many times abroad using aeroplanes, but never on a ferry, and I have to say that I was in love with the experience. It is like a mini cruise. You have your own cabin (ours was sparse, but I gather you can get better). There are shops on board with three levels of restaurant available; snacks, self service and fuck-off posh restaurant, complete with piano bar and waiter service. It was all in all lovely.

The boat pitched and rolled a little that crossing, but I have to say that it was such a lovely experience. If you have never travelled by boat, then you should. I remember as a teenager going on some manky school cruise in an old tub. Pulling out of Venice Harbour by boat was an experience I shall never forget as long as I live. The sight of Venice from the boat leaving the harbour as the sunset was priceless, even if the dinner aboard was stomach churning.

We had dinner, a few drinks and went to bed as Clara was feeling sick. The last thing I wanted on my hands was vomit. Poor old 'A' had to climb onto the top bunk, which was small. It you ever travel by ferry, then don't stint and buy a deluxe cabin, or don't bother at all and sleep on the floor. I shall come to that later.

I have to say that I fell asleep pretty quickly, and was only awoken by some strange music coming from somewhere that I couldn't place. It was pitch dark in the cabin (an inside cabin with no portholes – don't ever go there). It was so bizarre, that in my hazy half sleep I thought that my mobile phone, (or 'A's) had taken on some life of its own and decided to play music. It wasn't until after ten minutes of ferreting around in the dark that I realised it was the tannoy system of the ferry, announcing that all of its inhabitants should wake up as we were nearing the port. I wish they had warned us of that the night before. It would have saved me from a lot of post wine angst, and that of other passengers I am sure. Thankfully, it only disturbed 'A' for a few minutes, but that was too much as I ferreted about in the dark, while he kept saying "Joanne, what is that noise, is it your phone? Where is it coming from?" Still he had endured a night on a bunk that was five feet in the air and two feet wide; he is sixteen stone and 6'3. How he managed to sleep at all is beyond me.

The view of St Malo harbour as we docked was beautiful. It was a bright sunny day and the yachts moored in the harbour were bobbing up and down. The quaint old buildings lining the port were so pretty. The overall impression was of a well-heeled seaside town, not like some of the tacky ones we find at home in Britain.

After disembarking, we found our rental car that 'A' had booked in advance. It was a Fiat 'Up' and it is one of the smallest cars you can possibly imagine. After fixing the car seat that I had lugged all the way from the Midlands into the car we set off. Now, as a woman, I would have adjusted my seat and made myself familiar with the controls, but as 'A' is a man he did none of this. We lurched out of the port compound and straight onto French roads. Thankfully, everyone was heading in the same direction, and we managed to find our way out of St Malo. It was nerve-wracking for those first few miles as there was a quite a bit of traffic, but once out of the urban area things settled down; made easier by the fact that we were going in a straight line with relatively little traffic.

'A' had given me the map and I was in charge of map reading. It became a little tricky when we got on the motorway, as 'A' suddenly announced that he could see nothing in his wing mirror. He also said that he couldn't see how fast he was going, as the speedometer was obscured by the steering wheel and his knees which were wrapped around it. I acted as his eyes and told him whether cars were approaching or not as we left the slip road onto the motorway. At this point I was so stressed that I desperately wanted to light up a cigarette, but as it was a hire car that was impossible. I also had too much to do with being 'A's eyes, and trying to map read at the same time.

Clara was in the back asking if we could have the music on but I told her that "Dad was concentrating on his driving." This didn't go down well with the three-year old who wondered why dad was unaccommodating, unlike mom.

We did eventually, without too much difficulty, find our destination town of Lamballe and parked in the square. It was a Monday morning. We got out of the car in search of somewhere to have a snack and a cup of coffee.

Lamballe old town has a lot of medieval buildings. It was very quiet, but we did find a bar where we had a *croque monsieur*, a cup of coffee and used the rather unpleasant toilets. We then set off in search of our accommodation. We drove around for an hour, even going off the beaten track trying to find the place; all to no avail. A Fiat Up does not drive well on an unmade road. Tempers were getting frayed and I was trying my best to keep my patience with 'A' who was driving me nuts. I was also trying to keep Clara as entertained as I could because by now she was getting restless. In the end, we gave up and drove back to town where 'A' went to the tourist information office to see if they knew where it was.

I watched him walk back to the car across the car park with a stony face, and I held my breath.

He came back and announced that they didn't know where it was, but they had phoned the owner who was coming into town to rescue us. We could her follow her back to her place. I let out a sigh of relief.

When we got to the owners house, and her rather charming little Romany caravan parked right next to her field of free range chickens, it was pretty obvious that we would have never found the place without help. After establishing the internet connection and unpacking our bags we decided to go into town for some supplies for that evening's meal.

Despite having been in the town a few hours earlier, we had difficulty getting off the ring road that circled it, and back to the supermarket we had passed along the way out of town. We drove around that ring road three times in all, arguing all the way. In the end I kept quiet and it was only when 'A' ran a red light and glanced a curb, did I open my mouth to tell him he had done so. Apparently he hadn't noticed. We finally found the supermarket and we were both in bad humour with each other.

After a short, but quite vociferous argument in the supermarket, we grabbed our groceries and got back to the Romany caravan. It was only after several glasses of wine, that we were sufficiently calm enough to resume speaking to one another.

We were to be in Brittany for three nights. It was something of a tall order when looking for a property to buy. It was the supermarket sweep version of house hunting, but I am sure that we are not alone in this approach when looking to buy a property abroad. 'A' had three houses that he wanted to view, and the first viewing was arranged for the following morning. Desperate not to have a repeat of today's motoring tension, I went out to the little car and managed to adjust the seat for someone as tall as 'A'. I also adjusted the steering wheel. I looked at the map for the location of tomorrow's property and calculated how long it would take us to get there. I was going to be prepared if nothing else. I did not want a repeat performance of today's domestic skirmishes.

We set off a little after eight thirty the next morning, and travelled deep into the countryside; through a mountainous region full of pine forests. We finally found the little village where we were to rendezvous with the *immobilier* (estate agent).

I didn't like the town. It was like one of those sleepy Welsh villages in the middle of nowhere that hadn't seen a person outside of the locale in years. There was not a soul about and the only 'shop' in the village was a *tabac*. We *parked* in the village car park which was in front of the church, opposite the cemetery and waited. We were early so we sat in the car chatting, keeping a watchful eye for any car in the hope it was our man. We only saw two cars in the forty five minutes we sat there and only one person; a rather elderly woman who went into the cemetery.

The *immobilier* was late. He was very late. He clearly wasn't going to show. He had 'A's number, but his phone didn't ring. We decided to go for a coffee in the *tabac* before we set off. 'A' was angry that this was turning out to be a disaster.

The *tabac* was dark and dingy inside, and it was like stepping into a time warp. A stuffed fox head hung on the wall behind the counter, and there were various other dead stuffed animals on the walls around the room. The locals were clearly very into their hunting; that was apparent. We drank our coffee rather swiftly and got back in the car.

Chapter 3

We had another appointment scheduled for a little later in a town that was nearby. We just hoped this property would be better. Perhaps we may actually get to view one. I have to say again, that there was no one about in the town where the office was located, but at least it didn't look like something out of a horror film, as the village earlier had done.

A most charming middle-aged man came out of the *immobilier's* office and kissed me on both cheeks. We then followed him in his car to the property we were going to view. It was situated along a dirt track that branched off the main road, and was positioned on the side of the hill. There was a large garden with it, but nowhere near enough land for what 'A' had in mind. The biggest drawback in 'A's eyes was the fact that there were neighbours not fifty metres away from the property. 'A' wanted somewhere secluded and I was inclined to agree with him. There is no point in living in a rural area if you are going to have some other blighter living that close. But we still looked inside.

It was disappointing. There were two rooms on the ground floor which were badly in need of re-decoration, and they had pine cladding on the walls. That in itself was not a problem, but I suspected there were horrors waiting under the cladding. Then he showed us around the back of the house. It was bizarre to say the least. Whilst the ground floor was somewhat elevated, as you had climb a small flight of steps to access the front door, around the rear was the ground floor proper. It was what I can only describe as a half-cellar. There were hardly any windows, and the few that existed were located high up in the walls. In this room, which looked like a cross between a garage and a workshop was the bathroom. This comprised of a toilet and a bath from the early nineteen seventies judging by the avocado colour and the busy patterned brown tiles on the walls. I have no idea why they had chosen to locate the bathroom here, but I suspect it was the same reason that a lot of terraced two-up, two-down houses had their bathrooms tagged onto the backend of the kitchen; lack of available space. It looked like a torture chamber out of a horror film written by Stephen King, where someone would have been kept prisoner for years, enduring untold torture, until they finally managed to escape into the woods behind the building.

I tried very hard to keep an open mind about this house, and have some vision, but as much as I tried my imagination would not stretch to seeing this as a nice home. The place would have to be gutted first and that would be work.

We thanked the *immobilier* and climbed back into the car. "What do you think?" said 'A'.

"I am not sure," I replied, "what are your thoughts?"

"I don't like how close those neighbours are, but if I don't see anything else this trip, then I will put an offer in on it."

Oh God, it was worse than I thought. Was he actually so desperate that he would even consider this place? Apparently he was. Something had to be done.

Earlier whilst waiting for the *immobilier* that didn't show, I had studied the map. There was a large town nearby, and I suggested that we visit to have a look around. We could also grab a sandwich for lunch. Who knows? There just may be some *immobilier* offices with a dream property for sale that fitted his budget.

So we drove to the nearby town of *Carhaix Plouguer*. We left the forested scenery behind us, and as we approached the town the overall impression was more welcoming. It actually resembled civilisation. On our way into town we passed a Lidl and a large Le Clerc supermarket. There was, I also noted, a Point P builders merchants.

We found the main street and parked up near a sandwich shop that sold enormous baguettes. 'A' went in and purchased two for our lunch and we sat in the car eating them. We both liked the look of this town. There were shops on either side of the street and several bars. It looked as though the place was thriving. We decided to walk the length of the main street.

It was very pretty and well looked after. Bunting was threaded across the street which gave it a holiday atmosphere. We had a drink outside of a bar and it was all very nice. Sadly there were no properties in any of the *immobilier's* windows that fitted 'A's budget, so that turned out to be fruitless.

We drove back to the caravan after getting supplies at the supermarket we had visited the evening before in *Lamballe*. 'A' cracked open the wine, while I cooked the dinner. 'A' was talking about putting an offer in on the only property we had viewed as he had run out of options. I couldn't believe he was actually contemplating this and was keen to stop him. Then I had an idea. I asked him if he still had the particulars of the place near the canal, the one he had sent me months earlier in his emails, and did he know where the house was located?

He found the details and said that it was not far from *Carhaix Plouguer*. He did add that the *immobilier* had never got back to him. I suggested that perhaps the receptionist didn't speak English and had totally ignored the email.

The possibility of seeing that house was too tempting for me, so I suggested that we drive out to the *immobilisers* tomorrow and ask them if it was still for sale. Thankfully, with no other option available, 'A' went for the idea.

The next day we found the *immobilier's* office. I walked in and said "*Parlez vous Anglais?*" to the receptionist. 'A' was mortified that I had adopted such an approach, but I was not going to let that dream property slip out of our hands because of my inability to speak French.

It would seem that she didn't speak English but I managed to make myself understood, enough to communicate that we were interested in a property. She told us to come back after lunch.

This was when it hit us both that the French have two hour lunches. We had passed a small restaurant on the way to the offices, so we decided to go there for lunch. It was a set menu of three courses for 8.95 Euros. It certainly wasn't Raymond Blanc standards, but it was okay. What surprised us though was that there were workmen in there having a three course lunch with beer! Welcome to France.

Later we met Madame Le Lay and thankfully her English was good enough for us to make ourselves understood. We explained that tomorrow was our last day and that we urgently wanted to see the property in question. She arranged to meet us tomorrow afternoon. She gave us the address so that we could go there and look for ourselves.

The sun was shining, and we were both excited. So excited, that as we tried to find our way to *Cleden Poher*, 'A' nearly put the little car down the ditch at the side of the road whilst I was looking at the map. I would be relieved when this little trip was over, and we handed the hire car back. I am used to driving myself, not being a passenger and 'A''s driving left little to be desired.

We pulled into the village of *Cleden Poher*. It was a sunny afternoon, and the temperature was climbing. There was a beautiful little square with a road running through it, and a church that was ever so pretty. There was a *tabac*, a hairdressers and a *boulangerie*.

We finally found the little road that the house was on and pulled into the lane. We hadn't gone far when we came to the house. It was instantly recognisable from the photos. It looked even better than it had in the emails. I fell in love with it instantly, but said nothing.

"This is it. This is the house," said 'A' as he drove past. We went to the end of the lane and came to the river. There was a turning place, and a little picnic bench with a roof on; something I had never seen in Britain. How thoughtful of the French to do something like that. The river was in fact the Nantes Brest Canal and on that early May afternoon it was an idyllic spot. There were fields either side of the turning place. "These fields are part of the land that comes with the house," said 'A'. It was simply getting better and better; this was by far the best property we had viewed.

We drove back up to the lane and parked on the verge opposite the house. The sun was shining and the meadow in front of the house was just gorgeous.

We stood looking at the house. It was built of stone and had been re-roofed. It boasted a new slate roof with dormer windows. It had steps leading up to the front door, which is so indicative of Breton houses. There was an annexe with a tin roof to the right of the house, and further stone ruins beyond that. The house looked serene as it sat there in the late afternoon sun. I fell even more in love with it as I surveyed the land that adjoined it. I already had dreams of having a neatly mowed lawn and parking space for two or three cars where the hire car was parked.

"What do you think?" said 'A'.

"I think it is absolutely gorgeous, what about you?" He agreed it was fantastic. Everything about it was perfect. The location, the land and the house itself was enchanting.

We drove back to the Romany caravan full of excitement for the viewing the next day.

Chapter 4

Well, I can tell you that 'A's spirits had considerably improved as we cracked open the wine that evening and sat talking about the upcoming viewing. I was just relieved that we had managed to salvage the trip, and find a suitable property all within the space of three days. The thought of how unbearable 'A' would have been if we had to return without finding a suitable property, was just too much. Thank God we had found one; and wasn't it a beauty.

We drove to the coast the next morning to kill time as we weren't scheduled to view the house until 4pm. It was only an hour away, and we walked around the little town of *Le Faou* on the mouth of the estuary. We stopped at a bar and had a beer. It was pretty apparent from what 'A' was saying that he would buy the house providing no horrors lay in store for us when we viewed it that afternoon. We couldn't wait to view the house internally, and the wait seemed to take forever. The time dragged.

We were early for our rendezvous with Madame Le Lay and waited in the car park in the town square in front of the church. 'A' started to worry that she wouldn't show. But his fears were unfounded and she arrived on the dot of 4pm. We followed her down to the house. She got out a bunch of keys and opened the door. We waited with baited breath to see the inside. It was better than expected.

She explained that it was owned by a man who had emigrated to Canada years ago, but his siblings were still living in this area of France. He had planned to renovate the house and come back to live in *Cleden Poher* but age had got the better of him. Having family in Canada, he had abandoned his dream, and decided to sell his French home. It had been an old grain store. It had been re-roofed and dormer windows had been put in the roof. Downstairs was one large room with magnificent old beams and new floorboards had been laid up stairs. Downstairs a new floor had been laid and it had been tiled. There was a very large Breton style fireplace.

In order to access to the upstairs, we went up the flight of stone steps that were located outside, at the side of the house as there was no internal staircase. Madame Le Lay opened the door. The afternoon light shafted into the room. The upstairs was a beautifully large space with oak A-frames where the eaves of the roof came down to meet the walls, about a metre from the floor.

Not one to muck about, 'A' went straight in. "I want to buy it," he said to Madame Le Lay.

"Will you need a mortgage?" she asked.

"No, I have cash," he said. She looked suitably impressed. "But it is our last day here and I need to get it sorted today," he added.

"Come up to the *Mairies* office and we will sort it out." the impeccably dressed, young French woman said.

An hour later we were driving back to the caravan. 'A' had now purchased a property or at the very least had signed up to buy. We stopped off and bought a bottle of champagne to celebrate.

We had to be at the ferry by 8am the next morning, so celebrations were somewhat curtailed for an early night. I was so excited. But we had to catch that ferry in the morning.

We made it to the ferry just in time and by the skin of our teeth, having taken a wrong turn on the way back. It was a good forty minutes of anxiety I can tell you, and more than once I thought we wouldn't make it. I swigged the last of the champagne, straight out of the bottle on the car park when we handed the hire car back.

Once on board the ferry and in the gift shop, I vowed to get a Michelin map for our return journey to complete the purchase. We would not be having a repeat performance of today's nerve wracking journey back to the ferry. I felt in need of a bloody stiff drink, and it was only ten in the morning.

'A' went back to Saudi and emailed updates about his property deal. Everything was going to plan and he was scheduled to complete the purchase at the end of July. He purchased a touring caravan from an old British couple in Brittany and had arranged for them to deliver it to the house on the Sunday that we were due to arrive in France. We had decided to take my car this time, and 'A' sent me the money to purchase all the necessary stuff for our trip.

As a minimum legal requirement you need to have a GB sticker, a breathalyser kit, a high Vis vest and a warning triangle. Also you needed headlight stickers to convert your headlights for driving on the other side of the road. These kits are readily available on the internet and at a very reasonable price. You can buy them onboard the ferry, or at the ferry terminal, but they do charge a high price owing to the captive audience of disorganised people. I purchased a Michelin map from Amazon and plotted our route, writing down the road numbers we should take. I also had my V5 document and car insurance documents in an envelope in the glove box of the car (another pre-requisite).

I was quite excited about the trip and researched all that I could. The only downside about the trip was that it was the beginning of the summer holidays, and as such the ferry was booked to capacity, there were no cabins to be had. We would have to make do with lounge chairs to sleep on. As we would be arriving in France on Sunday, we would need to take some food as supermarkets and restaurants generally do not open in rural France on a Sunday; it is still largely a catholic country. Petrol stations would also be closed so we needed to make sure we filled up with petrol before getting onboard the ferry.

The day soon dawned when I was to collect 'A', from Manchester airport this time. I had set off early allowing plenty of time for the journey, but it was Friday afternoon and the traffic was bad. He was waiting outside when we pulled up. He was in a foul mood. I don't know why, but there was an aura of anger about him. I hoped it would pass.

I think it was just the combination of heat, a long flight and tiredness, as once back at my house he seemed to relax. The next morning after a good night's sleep his good humour was restored and we even went shopping for some clothes in the morning for him. He purchased a navy and white striped t-shirt, he laughed about it being very French. "All you need is a beret and a string of onions and you are all set," I joked. Of course, that is very stereotypical and I don't think I have ever seen a French man wearing a beret, yet alone a stripy t-shirt or a string of onions. By the way, if you didn't know, berets were worn by the Resistance during World War Two. Quite how the Germans didn't cotton on to this tell tale sign of the Resistance I don't know.

We set off for the Ferry at midday after stopping at Greggs for a pasty lunch and made it to Portsmouth in good time. We did fill up with petrol before we joined the queue for the ferry, which was packed with holiday makers in all kinds of vehicles with roof racks and cycle carriers. We still had ages to go until we boarded the ferry. We decided to do as a lot of others were doing, and leave the car to go into the terminal for a drink at the bar.

We were very much in holiday mood and after a pint for 'A' and a large glass of wine for me; we made our way back to the car. Much to my horror, my aged car seemed to have sprung a leak and there was petrol trailing from the car. I bent down to have a look but couldn't see where the petrol was coming from. 'A' had put the petrol in and the pump he had used didn't seem to want to cut off. He did remark at the time, "how much bloody petrol does your car hold as it is up to £60 already?" I think it was over filled and the petrol had spilled out of the baffle. I just hoped and prayed that that was all it was. The last thing I wanted was my car blowing up on the ferry half way across the English Channel.

The ferry started loading, and the queue inched forward. 'A' lit up a cigarette. "Whatever you do," I said "do not throw your butt end out of the window or we could all go up in a puff of smoke." Thankfully he didn't, and I was relieved to park the car and get out.

It is a very strange experience when you board the ferry in your car. Armies of Marshalls guide you up through the car decks, and you park your car in tightly packed rows. It was an eerie and quite claustrophobic experience. I did as instructed and left my car in gear, and turned off the car alarm. We left the car and got into the lift that took us to the main part of the ferry.

We went straight to the self service restaurant and joined the queue for dinner. It sounds grim but it isn't. Brittany Ferries is French and consequently so are most of the staff on board. In the restaurant, the chefs are dressed in chef's whites serving the food as you file past with your trays. 'A' and I opted for *beouf bourguignon*. Clara had a kids meal which comes with a goodie bag of little games and activities designed to keep your child busy. In this particular bag was a bundle of coloured plastic sticks. There were no instructions and neither 'A' nor I could make head or tail of what to do with them. Ah well, some things are beyond the comprehension of the over forties, we concluded as we left the restaurant and headed for the bar.

It was a lovely sunny evening as we stood on the deck at the rear of the ferry smoking a cigarette and looking out to sea. The boat was full, as was the bar and cabaret area. I could hear music coming from inside and my Clara started tugging frantically at my arm. I couldn't hear what she was saying, but followed her obediently into the bar. On the stage was a man dressed in a teddy bear costume and wearing a stripy t-shirt, he had a beret on his head. Well, at least the French can take the piss out of themselves. In fact as I have later discovered, they have quite a dry sense of humour. The bears name was Pierre le Bear and he makes a regular appearance on the ferry in the summer months.

I have to say that neither 'A' nor I are 'cabaret' type people, but to please our three year old daughter, 'A' suggested that we watch the cabaret. I found some seats while he went to the bar to get yet another bottle of wine. We needed to get pissed to sleep in those lounge chairs, 'A' had quite wisely said. It was going to be a long night.

Chapter 5

We found our allocated chairs at around 10pm and attempted to get some sleep. There were bodies littering the floor. Some of them even had sleeping bags. They had quite clearly done this before. I spent about an hour trying to get to sleep, before deciding that the floor was definitely better than a chair, and together with Clara we lay down in-between the seats so that we wouldn't be trodden on. Using my handbag as a pillow and my pashmina as a blanket, we did drift off to sleep, eventually.

I woke at 4am and couldn't get back to sleep. My hip was stiff from sleeping on the floor, but Clara was sound asleep thankfully, as was 'A', still upright in a lounge chair. I needed a cigarette so I tip-toed over to him. He was half asleep. I nudged his arm and his eyes opened. "Will you watch Clara while I go for a cigarette?" I asked

I quite enjoyed the peace and quiet of a ship full of sleeping travellers. I walked through the sleeping ship up to the helipad which was the only door open to the outside. I passed a couple of Brittany Ferry employees *in flagrante* on the staircase, but they were so absorbed with each other they didn't notice me.

An hour later, when I was back in my chair, I was rather sad when the inhabitants of the ferry all started to wake up. Prior to then, I had watched the dawn and listened to the slow rumble of the ferry's engines.

Slowly one by one they started to wake. My peace was shattered.

The ferry would be docking at 8am, and we had time to grab an outrageously priced takeaway tea and coffee before heading down to the car deck. It was honestly one of the worst cups of tea I have ever tasted in my life, and I vowed never to buy one on board a ferry again.

Despite the lack of sleep on the ferry we were in good spirits. 'A' complained bitterly about sleeping in the lounge seat. He said that he had hardly slept a wink, despite me watching him snore his head off for two and a half hours. I can only presume he was awake whilst I slept.

It was very quiet on the roads once we were away from St Malo. The drive was very pleasant. Surprisingly, I managed to remember the way without much trouble or needing to resort to asking 'A', who despite moaning about my map reading skills when he drove was no better than I was.

We arrived in the sleepy little village of *Cleden Poher* at about 11.30am. I had noted that there was no sign of supermarkets being open when we drove past one, so I was right in my statement that they generally don't open on Sunday. It was a good job that I had brought some food with me in a cooler box, although how long it would stay cool was anyone's guess, as the temperatures were soaring.

The middle-aged couple with the caravan were going to arrive at 1pm. 'A' had already paid them and was now worried they wouldn't show. I re-assured him that I thought they would, and we went and had a beer in the local bar opposite the church. We sat outside at a table on the pavement. 'A' said he felt the locals boring holes into him as they watched us. To be honest I can't say that I thought that at all. He was clearly very tired and anxious, which was probably not helping his paranoia. He purchased a bottle of wine from the tabac for that evening's meal and we went and waited in the car.

Sure enough, a car towing a caravan pulled around the corner of the square a little before 1pm and I recognised it as being the caravan in the photo. They followed us down to the house. 'A' had envisaged having the caravan sited near to the river, but the gentleman of the couple said he thought that it was a bad idea. He towed it up to the meadow opposite the house. The meadow had grown considerably since we were here at the end of April and it was now thigh high. 'A' had quite wisely purchased a petrol strimmer from the gent and the man kindly set about strimming the area where the caravan was to go. His wife chatted with me while their large hairy dog roamed about. The caravan was soon in place and we thanked the couple who went and parked down by the river to take their dog for a walk.

I must admit that I couldn't wait to get in the caravan and make a cup of tea. I pride myself on my organisational abilities, and this was no different. I had bought a camping kettle from Alde, and I had packed crockery, cutlery, mugs, utensils, some saucepans and a frying pan; washing-up liquid, tea towels, dish-cloths and scourers. I had bedding and towels, not to mention food in the cooler box, as well as supplies of tea bags, coffee plus other dried goods. I had planned spaghetti bolognaise for that evenings meal. I couldn't risk fresh meat going off in the cooler box for 36 hours so I had purchased a tin of ready prepared bolognaise sauce from Marks and Spencer. Tomorrow I would get supplies from the shops when they opened.

The water was 'hooked up' as the couple had kindly thought to bring some water with them, so I filled the kettle and placed it on the stove. I turned on the gas but nothing happened. I couldn't hear it hissing either. I went to the front of the caravan and to the locker to see if the gas was turned on. It appeared to be on, but I couldn't be sure. 'A' wasn't sure either and he had absolutely no experience of caravanning whereas I had. We decided to catch the couple as they returned from their walk. It was very hot and stuffy in the van and it smelled heavily of 'eau de dog', so we opened the windows. It wasn't a bad little purchase for 1600 Euros, and with a good clean and a strong air freshener to mask the smell of their hairy mutt, it would be okay.

We waited half an hour and their car was eventually heard and we flagged them down. I don't know what he did, but he managed to light the gas. Perhaps there was air in the pipe. Who knows, but I looked forward to a cup of tea.

'A' was not in a good mood. He was hot, and he hates being hot. It is bad enough that he has to work in 40 degree heat in Saudi Arabia, without sitting in a hot caravan without a breeze. He was also by now very hungry, which was adding to his irritation, so I decided to put the dinner on early and we cracked open the wine.

The dinner wasn't very wonderful, and 'A' moaned about it. Sometimes I find it hard to be patient with him, especially when he behaves like a small whiny child, but I kept my mouth shut. Tomorrow would be a better day, I assured myself and went to make 'A' a cup of coffee. But the gas didn't work. Oh dear, I thought to myself and went to the caravan locker. The pipe had come away from the regulator and it was held on by a jubilee clip. We didn't have a screw driver. 'A' blew a fuse, and we had a row. He decided that he wanted an early night.

I dutifully made up the large bed in the sitting area as this was only a two berth caravan. We were all going to sleep together. It was only eight o' clock and it was a lovely summer's evening. Thankfully both 'A' and Clara were soon fast asleep. I got out of bed and went for a walk down by the river.

It was beautiful. There was not a soul about. It was peaceful and tranquil. The surrounding countryside was stunning. The river was still, calm and serene as I walked along the tow path, and then back to the house. I poured the rest of the wine into my glass and sat on the steps of the house looking out across the meadow. I watched the sun sink lower into the sky, imagining the time when it would be turned into a garden, hopefully in the not too distant future. Looking back, I was clearly much too optimistic, but hindsight is a wonderful thing.

Chapter Six

I lay in bed unable to sleep, and thought about the gas pipe problem. The thought of not having a cup of tea in the morning was not a happy one, so I went outside to investigate, armed with a butter knife to use as a screwdriver. I fiddled about with the jubilee clip and did actually manage to attach the pipe back onto the regulator. Feeling very pleased with myself, I went to bed and attempted to sleep. I did drift off, but the duvet kept being pulled from me, leaving half of my body exposed to the now cold night air.

I must have slept because the next thing I knew it was morning. I cheerfully got out of bed and put the kettle on, feeling smug that I could boast that the gas was now working. Would 'A' like a cup of coffee? Well it was short lived. We did just manage to boil the kettle, but then the gas went out. When I went outside and looked in the locker the pipe had come off again. It must be the regulator. We would need to get a new one. I told 'A' the bad news. He was not happy as there would be no cooked breakfast for him. He was not happy. We had had the most fearsome of arguments on the way into town. It was bad that I threatened to dump him on the spot and drive straight back to the ferry. He finally shut up and said nothing for the remainder of the journey.

We finally managed to get into town to a supermarket, and once 'A' had stuffed a rather large breakfast pastry into his face, he was in a better mood. We perused the camping aisle of the supermarket. Alas, there were no regulators there. What we needed was a camping shop. It was frustrating to say the least.

Knowing the gas was not going to be sorted I bought some salad stuff for dinner and baguettes.

It was a very hot day. Not entirely wasted as we had to visit the *immobilier* in the afternoon to exchange contracts. After lunch, we had set off and got there on time. Now in France, the *immobilier* is the solicitor and estate agent rolled into one. It is quite convenient, and the buyer pays the estate agent fees. We all sat in a room around a large table and the *immobilier* (Madame Le Lay) and the seller were present. Well, the sellers aged sister who was acting as his representative. It was all very formal and I gathered from this that the French do like their bureaucracy. An hour later we stepped out into the afternoon. 'A' was now the proud owner of a house and land in France (albeit one that needed a lot of work). However, we were in a good mood and had the keys to the house. We went back and 'A' opened the door and then the shutters on the windows.

We spent a lovely evening sitting in the shade and cool of the downstairs of the house discussing the plans for the renovation. The next two days were spent working on cutting down some of the vegetation immediately outside of the house, and taking measurements. But the atmosphere was rather strained.

Without the gas we had no hot water or means of cooking. 'A' lit a fire in the house and expected me to boil a kettle on it 'camp style', but I was having none of it. Thankfully, the weather was hot enough not to need a hot meal, but I did want a cup of tea. I decided to go into town and buy a single gas camping ring for 10 Euros from the supermarket. At least we would have hot drinks. 'A' said he was not going to buy a camping stove when he had just spent 1600 Euros on a caravan, and cursed the seller for the whole time we were there.

It was not exactly fun, but I was confident that I could do something about the regulator problem once back home and had access to the internet.

We were plagued by flies in the caravan and spent our evenings swatting them with rolled up magazines; the free ones you get on Brittany Ferries that are designed to be like in flight magazines you get on an aircraft. At least they came in handy for something.

We had planned to go and meet the *Mairie* whilst we were there, and I put on make-up especially only to find that he was on holiday. Nearly six years later and we still haven't met the *Mairie*, despite numerous trips to his office, which also conveniently houses the post office. I am not sure he even exists.

I was relieved when we got back home and I had dropped 'A' off at the airport. But it was fun to do some research and have dreams about a house that was not mine. I purchased books from Amazon about renovating old houses, and living in France. I was going to be prepared if nothing else. My imagination whirred overtime, and the visions I had of that house being transformed were truly magical. It wasn't a fantasy. It could be achieved with a lot of hard work, and money. I was prepared for the hard work, and I rather relished the challenge.

I received a beautiful bouquet of Marks and Spencer's Sweet Avalanche pink roses and thought that 'A' was professing his love for me. He had been tetchy whilst we were in France, and had even broke down and sobbed on one occasion. I remained aloof. He had had his chance more than once and he had not made a move on me, so what the hell was the matter with him? When I told him how lovely the roses were, and asked him why he had sent them (I did this in an email), he told me that it was for emptying the porta-potti. I was crushed.

At the end of August, 'A' announced that he was jacking in his job and going to France to work on the house, and he asked if I would I go with him. Now lovely as this prospect seemed, I could just not up sticks and go to France. I lived in a rented house and it would mean giving up my tenancy. He also only had 16k, and I knew that this was not enough money. I tried to get him to stay on in his job until after Christmas, as this would give him over 20k. He would therefore have more money to play with, but he was having none of it, and said that he was coming back at the end of September.

We fell out; big time. I knew we would, as I wouldn't go out to France. We had nearly come to blows about how he was going to renovate the house in August via email and Skype, as our plans differed greatly. I wanted the kitchen in the annexe, and he said he wasn't going to touch it yet. The annexe presently had a tin roof on it and needed a new floor. Looking back, I think he was wise not to want it in the annexe as the money would go quicker than anticipated, but I had grand designs at the time. I was also cross about him giving up his job.

On a practical level, I thought that with the winter approaching, and no source of heating, lighting or running water, he was making life very difficult for himself in trying to start renovations then. Surely it would be better to wait until the spring? Apparently not it would seem.

'A' bought a cheap four-by-four car and he booked his ferry. He wanted me to go with him, but after our arguments and the things he had said, I decided against it. He had little or no idea how difficult it was going to be, and the gas debacle was still painfully at the back of my mind. I could imagine that is what it would be like, if I went out with him now. However, I did promise to go out once he was settled. I remember thinking to myself that he would be glad to see me after several weeks of trying to battle on his own and not getting very far.

He was going about it all the wrong way, and I wanted to tell him so. But men generally don't listen to the advice of a woman. It was infuriating to say the least.

'A' did have a mobile phone, but there was no signal at his house, so we communicated via email when he went into town and used the wifi at the supermarket or at McDonalds, where he seemed to spend a lot of his time. So far we were having an Indian summer, and the weather was good. I decided to go out and pay him a visit.

He had become friendly with his neighbours at the lockkeepers cottage and they had been very kind to him. They were retired and 'A' told me how his French was getting better. He asked if I would bring out some marmalade for them and that he had ordered the trees for the orchard, all thirteen of them at the cost of 200 Euros.

I am glad this was via email and not Skype, as he couldn't see my eyes rolling at the folly of spending 200 Euros on an orchard when so much needed doing to the house, but it wasn't my money. I booked my ferry up for the 30th October. I did not book the return journey.

I got busy and I went to IKEA and bought a few things to take with me. I had also purchased a porta-potti as 'A' had said he had vacated the caravan and was now living in the house. He had not got the gas working on the caravan and said it was too cold in there. I thought this was rather odd, as surely the caravan would be more comfortable than the house given its present condition. If the gas was fixed he would be warm in there and have facilities for showering and cooking, thus avoiding the necessity of buying a cooker. So much for his "I'm not spending 10 Euros on a camping stove when I have spent 1600 on a caravan." He had now spent over 100 Euros on a cooker instead of fixing the problem with the gas on the caravan. I did have to laugh inwardly at this act of hypocrisy.

He had also spent money on buying a second-hand bed frame and something to sit on downstairs, as well as a fridge (again, there was one in the caravan) and he had ordered some logs. He had also bought a wood burning stove which was due to arrive after I was due to arrive from England.

However, I would soon see what the conditions were like when I got out there.

Chapter 7

The weather was still warm during the day when I arrived, although it got dark early, and very cold at night. He was grateful for the things I had purchased and paid me for them. On the day I arrived he was having the electricity connected. Apparently his neighbour friend knew an electrician, and although the house needed re-wiring, the electricity board had agreed to supply some low voltage electricity to help him renovate the house. He had also, with the help of his neighbour, rigged up some pipe to the stop tap outside so that he had some form of running water. This necessitated going outside and turning on the stop tap to fill water containers with the aid of the pipe for use inside the house. He was using the water container from the caravan, but to my horror, he was also using the black water containers, totally oblivious that they had been used for waste water. I was not only shocked; I was surprised that he hadn't got ill.

The electricity board arrived with a flourish in the lane. It was a large truck complete with four work men. All of them fine young Frenchmen. I was in awe of their efficiency as they scaled the nearby electricity pole and were in and out of the house like the proverbial rats up a drain pipe. The electricity was connected within an hour, albeit just enough to run the fridge, a kettle and couple of table lamps. Looking back, I think 'A' had envisaged staying there for some time. Quite how long he thought his money would last, I don't know. But I knew it wouldn't last long.

Apart from cooking 'A' a full English breakfast on his new cooker with the sausages and bacon I had brought from England accompanied with his much loved brown sauce, I can't recall what we did that day apart from visit his neighbours. He gave them the marmalade that I had brought at his request, and that was a stilted affair. I noticed they had tiled floors throughout their lovely little lock-keepers cottage. I later realised it was because of the floods. But at the time I thought it was Spartan.

I do remember being shocked about the staircase he had started to build inside of the house. 'A' had bought a large amount of oak planks when he was in England that he had planned to use to make the staircase and whatnot (whatever the whatnot was). He had spent a good deal of time sawing, planing and routing this damn oak to make that staircase. It looked like a bloody ladder and it still wasn't finished. We still had to use the outside stone steps to get upstairs to bed.

The problem with the stone steps outside was that a) they were covered in moss and b) there was no hand rail. With a three year old child and having a fear of heights I was not a happy woman I can tell you. I had seen that moss and I do recall that one of the first things I did was to find an implement (I think it was from the fire companion set) to scrape the moss off. If it rained overnight those steps would be lethal. How it had not occurred to him to scrape the moss off I don't, know but I guess that is me just being 'pedantic'.

Aware that there was no lighting in the house (now better but still minimal thanks to the electricity board) I had taken out a large quantity of push button LED lights and cheap batteries. These came in very handy and I used them on the bedside table and as a torch when I needed to go downstairs to make a cuppa.

We slept in 'A's double bed. He had purchased this horrid, old, brown wooden bed-frame from Ty-recoup and a new mattress, albeit a cheap one. As there was a leak in the roof, (and 'A' had decided to place the bed directly under the leak instead of anywhere else in the large and available space), he had decided to keep the polythene on the mattress. With our daughter in between us, and the winter duvet I had thankfully brought out with me, it was as good as it gets. I say that, because I was perched on six inches of bed and was kept awake by cold draughts and the sound of the polythene on the mattress 'crinkling' with our every move.

The wind was blowing that night, I remember vividly because the large wooden door at the top of the outside staircase kept making a noise. It was warped and didn't fasten easily. In addition to that, the glass light above it had long ceased to exist, and in its place was some chicken mesh and bubble wrap. The wind was howling through it, and with the door banging it was quite eerie.

Now 'A' had been sleeping up there for some time; or had he? The thought occurred to me later that he may have only just moved out of the caravan prior to our arrival, because surely he would have done something about that bloody door. Now I come to think of it, he had an army camp bed next to the bed, which he said was for Clara.

With the low temperatures at night, the gaping hole in the floor where the half finished staircase was supposed to come up, and the lack of light, I took one look and said "she will sleep in between us" and that was the end of the camp bed. If he was trying it on with me he would have to do a lot better than that; although, as I said earlier, I didn't realise this at the time. It was not an obvious 'come-on'.

We must have managed to sleep (due to the cheap and good quality red wine), as we were awoken at five by what I can only describe as 'the hounds of the Baskervilles'. Notice I use the plural; hounds. Those dogs were barking like hell and baying as well. I couldn't make out if they were close by, or across the river. Still, it was unnerving enough. They sounded as though they hadn't been fed for a week. Their pitiful cries were haunting to say the least.

It was still dark. Thankfully, Clara was snug as a bug in a rug in between us, and was still fast asleep. 'A' was at least gallant enough to go downstairs to make a hot drink, having also been disturbed by the dogs barking. I could hear him messing about downstairs once he had unlocked the front door.

As I lay there in the dark with my pyjamas, a bathrobe and a pair of socks on I wondered what I had let myself in for. Why exactly had I come to this? I think I expected too much. My father was a builder, and he would have sorted this place out in no time at all. 'A' had not even managed to set up 'base camp' yet. I say that, because it was very much like a mountaineering expedition. There was the unknown out there and we had one bloody hell of a large mountain to climb.

Still it was morning and although the dogs hadn't stopped barking 'A' had made it back up the outside stone steps with a cup of tea for me. I was grateful not to have to do it myself. I had lit one of the large church candles I had bought out with me. It seemed most respectful and the right thing to do at the time, as those cheap batteries wouldn't last long in those LED lights I had purchased from the pound shop.

In one of those rare moments that you get with another human being, we sat and talked in the candle light. It was nice to be able to talk without a three year old butting in all of the time, and I was thankful that the bloody dogs had stopped barking. Or had they let them out to eat some poor unsuspecting creature in the woods? I put that thought to the back of my mind as 'A' talked about what he had planned for the day.

"We can pick up the trees for the orchard today." He announced gleefully. My heart sank. "I would like to get them planted as soon as possible, because the weather is set to turn soon. In a couple of days heavy rain is forecast." He said without turning a hair. My heart sank further. Now I knew the real reason for his desire in asking me to come. He wanted me to help dig the holes for the trees.

Now I pride myself on my gardening abilities, I really do. But 'A' and I were at loggerheads at over where this orchard should be sited. I had said that the meadow furthest away, by the river should be the place, as there was plenty of space there. He said that his neighbour, Pascal had said it should be up on the top of the hill, in the meadow that was hilly, because of the floods once a year. I did state that trees still grew down in the meadow by the river in spite of the floods, but it would seem that he was willing to listen to his neighbour who he had known for a mere five minutes over me.

That was the last place I would have put them. And yet, despite my years of gardening wisdom, 'A' would not change his mind. Up at the top of the hill they should go. I was too tired and weary to put up any kind of complaint. It was his land and his money, and if that is where he wanted them, then there they should be placed.

It was a cold damp start to the day, but the weather promised to get better as we set off the plant nursery or *Pepiniere* as it is called in France. 'A' insisted on using the French word whenever he spoke of it. I think he thought, by saying it in French, it made him appear as though he was fluent. In fact he prided himself on his French. It was short lived however, because he hasn't seemed to progress very far with it and now nearly six years later he is no better.

When we arrived we soon found the owner and 'A' spoke to him in French, although it was slow and stilted. I think 'A' had envisaged just collecting the trees and putting them into the back of his Honda CRV and driving off, but the nursery owner was having none of it, and insisted on giving us a pruning lesson; in French, of course.

He was a man about our age, with a rugged weather beaten face that one only gets by spending a large part of one's life outdoors. As he started to give us the lesson on pruning, he kept looking at me and saying "*oui*," just to make sure that I understood. I nodded in all the right places, but I knew how to prune a tree before this little demonstration. I just thought I would let him get on with it and give me a 'refresher course' as it were. He obviously loved showing off. He did say that if there was anything we needed, (although he looked at me and not 'A') to give him a call. I think he fancied me, but I was wearing my wellies and what my daughters called my 'Inspector Gadget' mac at the time. I didn't think that I looked very alluring. He must have been desperate that is all I can say, or had some strange penchant for middle-aged English women in macs and wellies.

We loaded all 13 bare rooted fruit trees into the back of the car and set off home. I had bought some gardening equipment out with me as I thought I would be cutting down some vegetation, but I hadn't envisaged planting trees so I had no spade. "We can make a start on planting them tomorrow," said 'A', "Pascal has given me a pick, as he said the ground up there is very stony."

Surely his neighbour was having a laugh. Why did he think that is was a good place to plant the trees if it was so stony? Surely wasn't that an indication that the land there was very dry? Or was it his idea of a sick joke? I can just imagine what he said to his wife, "Ah, that stupid Englishman doesn't know anything about gardening. I have told him to plant his trees at the top of the hill. I have given him a pick. That lazy shit has done nothing for weeks; now let's see him to do some work for a change." They must have had a right old laugh to themselves.

I wasn't laughing. "Have you got a spade A?" I enquired casually.

"No," he replied. "We had better go into *Carhaix* after lunch and get one."

Chapter 8

I thought it prudent to advise 'A' that he needed stakes for the trees as we drove into town to get the spade. This sent him into a fearful mood. "This orchard is turning out to be very expensive, what with the cost of the trees, a spade and now stakes. Is there anything else we need?" He said sarcastically.

"Some ties to tie the trees to the stakes." I said quietly. I didn't have the audacity to point out that I thought the idea of planting an orchard when he had only just made a start on the house and didn't even have a toilet, was sheer stupidity, but I kept my mouth firmly shut.

We went to the supermarket after 'A' had spent another 50 Euros at Mr Bricolage. He kept grumbling about money. So I purchased a rabbit for dinner that was reduced to half price, in an attempt to look like I was practising frugality out of respect for his diminishing funds. We got back to the house at about 3.30pm and I was aware that the light was fading. Inside of the house the light quality was poor, with only one table lamp to use as light in addition to the church candles I had brought out with me from IKEA. They look nice, but they don't give off much light even if you have got half a dozen of them. I hastily prepared dinner and put the rabbit on to stew.

It was cold, and it got colder when the sun went down. 'A' had purchased a load of logs before I had arrived and had made a little fire in the fire place. There was no grate and the fireplace; despite being huge didn't draw very well. There was an overwhelming smell of wood smoke in the room. The fire was making no difference to the temperature in the room whatsoever. I looked over at the fire and I could see why. He had only got five logs on there. No wonder you couldn't feel the heat from it. The room was 9 metres by 8 metres. Five logs were not going to cut the ice.

I went over and threw another four logs on the fire and was promptly told off by 'A'. "Don't put so many logs on the fire." He said rather sternly.

"But it is cold." I replied.

"It doesn't make any difference how many logs you put on there, it doesn't get any warmer," he said. I couldn't see the logic in this at all. If nine logs didn't get any hotter than four logs, which weren't giving off any heat at all, then why bother having a fire in the first place? He may have felt a little heat as he was sat right over the fire warming his hands like some character out of Dickens, miser that he was; while I was over by the cooker on the opposite side of the room, some eight metres away freezing to death. My patience was being sorely tested.

Another night was passed with the door banging, the wind howling and the dogs barking.

Next day it was promising to be a sunny day, but it was November and the mist hung over the meadow opposite the house in the early morning and stayed there until 10am. It is the river effect, and I have seen it many times before at the River Severn near Astley Burf. Today was going to be the day when we made a start on the orchard. Clara and I walked down the lane and up the steep hill to where we were going to site the orchard. 'A' drove up in his Honda CRV. He did offer us a lift, but as I was unsure of his driving abilities up a steep hill, I declined.

We set out the trees; a walnut, four apples, four pears and four plums. I could tell that 'A' was not looking forward to the manual labour bit. "How are we going to do this?" he said to me, "you are the gardener out of us." I don't know how he had the gall to say that after he had refused to listen to my advice about the sighting of the orchard instead preferring to listen to Pascal. Didn't the pick tell him something? I kept calm.

"I think I will go around to the holes and get the turf off first, and then you follow on using the pick to loosen the soil, then I will follow up and dig out the spoil." I said and added, "I am not big or strong enough to swing a pick."

He agreed to my suggestion, only, I think because I flattered his vanities about the 'big and strong' bit. It was hard going but I got into the swing of it. I could hear 'A' huffing and puffing behind me at the place I had just been. "The ground is bloody hard," he said, stopping to wipe the sweat from his forehead and take off his sweater. I had a little laugh to myself. I was quite enjoying myself up there on the brow of the hill with a view over the valley. It was a beautiful autumn day and you could see right down the valley for miles from up there. It would make a great spot for a picnic on a summer's day. It was not unpleasant either, it was warm and the sun was out. I carried on removing the top layer of turf from the places we had marked for the trees.

We hadn't seemed to be working for very long when 'A' said, "I need a break let's have some lunch."

I wasn't wearing a watch. "What time is it?" I called over.

"Nearly midday," he said. We hadn't eaten breakfast until after 9am and I don't think we must have started work until well after 10, I know that because the mist had cleared from the meadow when we walked up the lane. We had probably only done an hour's work.

I assessed the situation. He was tired and needed a break. "We haven't long had a cooked breakfast," I said.

"I don't care, I am knackered and I need a break." He said. I reluctantly agreed to have a break. We could have a quick lunch and then get cracking again, or so I thought.

He lingered over that lunch for an hour and a half, and it was only a baguette and a hot drink although he hung it out by saying he wanted another cup of coffee and a cigarette. I was growing impatient with his procrastination. "We had better crack on soon, "I said, "Because it gets dark at half past four and I have to get the dinner on before then, as I can't see what the hell I am doing in here in this poor light."

After another twenty minutes we went back up to the meadow and resumed the planting. It was taking us about twenty to thirty minutes to dig a hole and plant a single tree. The ground was very hard and stony and the work back breaking. We knocked off at 3.30 and went back to the house. Neither of us was in a very good mood. 'A' was knackered by having to do some manual labour for a change, and I was pissed off with him. Needless to say we had an argument that night when we went up to bed. He was picking at me for all sorts of silly things, the logs on the fire, the expense of it all, but there was something else that was the real cause of his annoyance and as usual he wouldn't say what it was; it was frustrating as well as annoying. The argument culminated with me telling him that if he required my help the next day that it would cost him £15 per hour. I then blew out the candle and went to sleep. After all, I was not only helping digging the holes, I had a three year old to look after and I was doing the cooking.

The next morning, I made him a cup of coffee and took it to him in bed, by way of an olive branch. I think he was somewhat surprised when I said about getting on with planting the orchard. "I thought you wanted paying," he said.

"Since when did you take any notice of what I say," I replied, and nothing more was said about the argument the night before.

After breakfast went down the lane to the meadow and resumed the planting. 'A' was clearly aching from the day before, but after last night's little 'set too' he quite wisely said nothing. We finished planting the orchard just in time, because the next day the weather turned.

Chapter 9

'A' had decided that for central heating, he was going to use a log burner with a back boiler, that heated the water, and he had ordered one from England. It was being delivered that morning. I was excited at the prospect. It was being delivered by the man who sold them and his 'assistant'. I am not quite sure what else to call her, because she was young, too young to be his wife, surely? Now I know you are thinking to yourself that it is no crime to have a much younger wife, and it isn't, except that the man in question was nothing to write home about. Having said that neither was his 'wife' if that is what she was. I did not enquire.

It was huge and quite heavy but they managed to get it up the stone steps at the front of the house with a little help from 'A' and myself. It sat in the middle of the room downstairs in its polythene wrapper. I was impressed. I offered them a coffee and we chatted about where it was to go; the fire place. The problem with the fire place was, that it had originally been open on all sides, but the previous owner had seen fit to fill in the sides, and to some extent the front with breeze blocks, and we didn't know why. Were they acting as some form of structural support for the massive chimney breast above? It was a conundrum that 'A' couldn't get his head around. I have come to realise that 'A' does a lot of thinking about jobs before he actually does them. This drives me nuts.

We waved the couple off and were left with the log burner in the middle of the room. I asked if he had sorted out someone to fit it, but it seemed that he hadn't got that far yet.

'A' suggested that I make a steak and ale pie for dinner, as that was what he wanted, and he also suggested that I make one for his neighbours at the lock-keepers cottage. I thought this was a terrible idea. We had no sanitation, no running water and we lived in a hovel. I wouldn't accept a pie from someone in those circumstances, but I didn't offer an objection, I just went along with it. There were a number of obstacles to overcome in making a pie. We didn't have a pie dish, or weighing scales and I didn't have any recipe books with me. 'A' was convinced that he still wanted a pie (I think he wanted to show case my culinary skills to the neighbours) so we went to the supermarket to buy a pie dish and weighing scales. Now the problem when you first move to a foreign country is that you don't know where to buy things cheaply and he ended up paying through the nose for the pie dish and the weighing scales. He moaned about it all the way back to the house.

Extreme cooking, that is what I called it. I used an empty wine bottle as a rolling pin and the top of the wood burner as a work surface, and even though I guessed the flour to fat ratio, I felt I had made a pretty good job of those pies (because I did indeed make two as asked). Michelle and Pascal stopped by in the afternoon to see how we were doing. Michelle wanted to see the electric lights in the house. 'A' asked them if they would like a steak pie. They declined politely, as I knew they would. This stuck in 'A's craw, as he brought up the cost of the items he had purchased to make those bloody pies. I could have hit him with my wine bottle rolling pin.

It started to rain and it turned cold. I felt helpless as he wanted to do everything his own way, and would not listen to suggestions. As far as I could tell, he had spent a lot of money on a lot of tatty furniture, made a start on the staircase (which was not finished so we couldn't use it) and had not really done a lot of work. My patience was wearing thin and it was very cold in the house, not to mention dark. It certainly wasn't suitable for a three year old and after ten days I was beginning to look at ferries to return home. Things were brought to a head rather rapidly as one Sunday evening Clara slipped in McDonalds and banged her head on the toilet door causing a rather nasty gash. We argued that evening as he did not want to take her to A and E (it later transpired that he was afraid the authorities would be called and find his sanitation lacking and he would face a fine). I had a sleepless night fretting over Clara and we left for the ferry first thing in the morning. My tyres screeching as I drove away from the house.

I went straight to see the doctor on board the ferry as soon as we were aboard. God only knows what he must have thought as we both smelled of wood smoke from the open fire, and hadn't had a shower for over a week. I just hoped that he thought I was 'eccentric'. Thankfully, Clara was alright, although she still bears the scar to this day on her forehead and I will never forgive him for it.

It took a long time before we spoke again.

He remained in France and I had periodic emails from him. I can't say that I had any sympathy for his plight. The staircase still wasn't finished, as he said it was too cold for the wood glue to set. He had started plaster boarding upstairs and was making a pair of French doors to replace the external door to the second floor that was repaired with chicken wire and bubble wrap. Apparently, he had found something to make them with at Ty Recoup. Why he just didn't go out and buy a pair was beyond me, like the staircase. The man hours he was spending on these jobs that he had no prior experience in was ridiculous. The house would never be renovated at this rate.

Then in January he went quiet. I didn't hear from him for several weeks. It was quite worrying. Michelle and Pascal had given up their summer residence of the lock-keepers cottage sometime shortly after I had left and had moved into their apartment in *Carhaix*. 'A' didn't see a soul for days. He had no credit on his mobile phone, and the signal was sporadic at the house. He was plaster boarding the inside of the roof upstairs in the house, and he was using a ladder. I had visions of him falling and lying injured for days. I had tried phoning him, but there was no answer. I was on the verge of phoning the local *Marie* when he replied to one of my many "Are you okay? I am worried," emails I had sent. He had indeed fallen from the ladder and had hurt his ribs. He had been in so much pain that he had retired to bed to heal. Thankfully, I had left my medical kit behind with an emergency stash of codeine, which he had been taking.

He came back to England in the April for a brief visit. Well that is what he had said it was to be. After a few days it transpired that he had no money left and wanted to doss at my house. I politely said 'no' as he would jeopardise my tenancy. My landlord lived next door and saw all that went on in my house. I knew this would happen. He had achieved very little with his £16k and now his money had run out. He did manage to get his brother to lend him some money and he went back out to France again. I just shook my head and tutted. He still hadn't had the leak in the roof fixed or had the log burner installed.

He came back in the summer, bringing the caravan with him for me to have in lieu of maintenance he hadn't paid. He had a job abroad and was going out to it in September.

Within the space of three weeks I had fixed the gas regulator, cleaned it from top to bottom and sold it for £1300.

Chapter 10

The next couple of years went by without much happening. 'A' did go abroad but only for a few months. He went to Oman and then jumped to Iraq where he had worked before. It was still very unsettled and rather dangerous and I wasn't surprised, when at the end of January the following year he had jacked it in and was back living with his mother in Wales. I was struggling to get a job myself, and was rather angry with him about giving up that job in Saudi. Not to mention wasting the £16k on fannying about. I was struggling to get by, and without his maintenance it was bleak. We had periods when we didn't communicate with one another. He was on a downer and I had no sympathy given that I was struggling. I do recall one of the times we did speak on Skype he said that it was okay because he had 10 years to do up the place in France. He had no sense of urgency at all. I pointed out that he had no idea what was around the corner, and he could get sick and unable to do the work needed on the house.

He got a job in UAE and it lasted all of two months. When I met him again after many months of not seeing him, I was surprised at how unfit he was. He was overweight (he had never really liked exercise and he ate the wrong foods and too much of them) and he got out of breath quickly. He admitted he needed to do something about it and then in 2017 he had a massive heart attack and had to have a stent fitted into a major artery. His life was never going to be the same again. My heart went out to him, but he would not accept any help from me whatsoever.

He said he wished that he had died. He had to give up smoking and he would be on medication for the rest of life. He went into a massive depression and couldn't see the wood for the trees. He also was very bitter about Brexit. Nothing I could say or do made any difference and most of the time he turned on me. He was seriously unpleasant to the point that I cut him off. Months of trying to help, months of trying to lift his mood, and all he could do were to be nasty. I had had enough. I wasn't having the best of times myself and was struggling to look after Clara and my unemployed son who lived with us. We didn't communicate for nearly twelve months.

But time is a great healer and I felt sad that he hadn't seen Clara. It wasn't right and I felt despicable for letting things get to the state that they had, although in my defence I just found it so draining to deal with his depression and constant negativity. So I sent him an email and offered him the olive branch. I fully expected him to send a vile and vicious email back, but to my surprise he didn't. He was actually quite civil. It was now February 2019.

We arranged to meet and he was very pleasant and certainly in a lot better place than he had been previously. He had been working abroad and had amassed some money. He said he would not be going back to his mothers. He had a job in Saudi in the pipe line and he was just waiting on the visa; given the formalities which the Saudi's insist on is rather a lot. He had to have his qualifications verified and he seemed to think that this would take months. He probably wouldn't go out to Saudi until August.

I had travelled to Wales to see him on that cold February Sunday, and as we sat in a bar feeling content from the Sunday lunch we had just eaten, he told me about how he had been out to Le Stêr the previous summer for a couple of weeks.

He had arrived in Paris by plane and caught the train to *Carhaix*. Apparently his posh neighbour Julien had collected him from the train station. Julien had been a big cheese in Caterpillar (if I remember right) and was now retired. He lived on the opposite side of the river in an old Mill house that had been extensively renovated. It is beautiful by all accounts, although I have never been inside. 'A' said it was contemporary and not to his tastes. He prefers old and rustic. I like a mixture of both, as done right it can have spectacular results.

He said that he hadn't done any work on the house as he had been there on holiday. The mice had nibbled at his mattress, and he had found an owl, dead on the floor of his bedroom. Apparently he hadn't discovered this until he had woke the morning after arriving. How you can miss a ruddy great dead owl on the floor of your bedroom I don't know. It must have fallen down the chimney and unable to get out had died. He felt very sad about it, and had taken it as an Omen. I think it more likely, that the poor old bird was ill and fell off his perch at the top of the chimney, ultimately to his death.

He told me that this year was all about completion for him, and he had just completed the Camino, a walk that he had started some years earlier. He was thinking about going out to France until his visa for Saudi came through.

He had £16k (again, what is it with £16k?). Without thinking I said that I would go with him.

I had always regretted not being able to go out to France for any length of time before as I had commitments. Now I didn't really have any. I was not in employment as I had started to publish my books and I was living with my eighty year old father. I didn't have to pay rent or bills. I would have to take Clara (who was by now eight years old) out of school, but quite honestly it would only be for a term and she could go to school in France. It would be the right time of year, and it would be an opportunity to see what life would be like living in France; something I had always dreamt of. It is one thing having a dream, it is quite another to live it and I could absolutely hate it. This way, I could see if I really did like it. It would also give 'A' the opportunity to spend some time with his daughter.

'A' immediately agreed, and said he would give me 100 Euros a week for food. I got very excited about the prospect.

'A' moved to a B & B in Bridgnorth, and set about finding a van to go out to France in. I applied for a passport for Clara, which would take a few weeks to obtain. Within four days he had purchased a van and had booked his ferry for the 14th March. I would probably not be able to go out until after the Easter holidays, as the ferry prices rise dramatically during the school holidays.

I had lots of stuff that 'A' could take with him in his van, but it all happened so quickly I didn't have time to get it together. I was rather annoyed, especially as 'A' said that he would pay for us to go out on foot (cheapskate that he is). As usual with most men, (sorry blokes for this sweeping generalisation, as I am sure you are not all like it) he had made plans in his head, and had failed to communicate them, expecting me to mind read. His main reason for departing so swiftly was that it would save the expense of the B&B, although a few extra days would have meant he could have taken all sort of stuff out with him that would have been helpful, and saved further expense in France. But he didn't see it like this. So he left. I did manage to give him an electric blanket that I had bought for my father the Christmas before, which he had politely, but firmly refused.

Chapter 11

We emailed each other when he went into *Carhaix* to the supermarket and to do his washing. This was twice a week. He kept asking me if I had received Clara's passport, and had I booked my ferry. I couldn't book the ferry without receiving the passport, but he didn't seem to think this a good enough reason.

He was downloading films at the supermarket cafe, using their internet so that he could watch them back at the house. He wasn't doing any work, and he was getting up late. It was still rather cold, and he admitted that he had totally forgotten about the electric blanket I had given him. He had only discovered it two weeks after arriving in France. 'Fuckwit' I thought. This was not good, and I predicted that his mood would descend pretty quickly under such harsh living conditions, which it did, rapidly.

One of the things he had wanted to achieve was to have the wood burner installed. I thought that this was an excellent idea that would improve the living conditions at the house dramatically, and improve his quality of life there. Three weeks after he had arrived in France he phoned me via Skype, and despite his email moniker, he was not a happy bunny. He was having no luck in finding someone to fit his log burning stove, although he hadn't put much effort in on that score. He had gone to a showroom in *Carhaix* and had been told that they only fitted log burners that they supplied. They had given him a number of someone in the area that fitted them, but he said that he had been unable to contact them. It was time for me to take action.

It is difficult to do anything these days without the internet. Searching for goods to buy, pricing comparisons or finding any services is made so much easier using the internet. If you live in the UK, we have excellent internet for most of the time. Some rural areas have difficulties but it is nothing like France. France is a very large country and there are a lot of rural areas. In most of the rural areas there is no internet although I gather that President Macron has vowed to change this over the next few years. In a country where most rural areas are not on mains drainage, and a lot of properties still have old, inadequate or non-existent sewerage systems, I think that hoping they will all have access to high speed broadband is rather optimistic but we shall see.

The house in France is about a mile from the village of *Cleden Poher*. *Cleden Poher* is located at the top of the hill and *Le Stêr* (that is then name of the house) is down in the valley, by the river. Apart from *Le Manor* about 500 metres up the road, and the lock-keepers cottage about 500 metres in the opposite direction, the only other houses are Julien's former Mill house and another house further along on the opposite side if the river. Despite being in his seventies, Julien has moaned about the lack of internet in that area for a long time. Now, if anyone can get the internet put on, it is Julien. He has connections, influence and money but it still doesn't help. There is still no sign of broadband down at the bottom of the hill. They are still using satellite to gain access to the internet.

Because of this, I decided that I had to help 'A' as much as I could whilst I was in the UK, and I have excellent broadband. I was in the middle of editing, but I put that task on the back burner and searched for log burner installers in Brittany. I immediately came up with two, both English. This was a good sign and I looked at the Face book page of one of them, as neither had a website. I promptly sent him an email enquiring about fitting 'A's wood burner. The other installer didn't have much information or a professional Face book page, but I did have an email address, so I emailed him as well.

Years earlier, we had toyed with the idea of installing the log burner ourselves. We had read all about it and 'A' had even purchased the flue, together with other bits and pieces and a chimney pot. I had found an excellent website run by a man who has many years in installing wood burning stoves, and I was delighted to find that his website had full instructions and was clearly laid out. The only stumbling block was getting on the roof. I have a fear of heights and get petrified when I get about ten feet off the ground. Climbing a ladder is a nightmare scenario to me.

Although the chimney was at a considerable height from the ground at the front of the house, you could easily walk around the back and climb onto the roof. The house backs onto the land behind it, which is as high as the roof. Over the years, leaves and soil erosion has filled in the gap that was once there, to the point that you can now walk around the back of the house and step onto the roof quite easily. Now, a younger person would have no problem getting up to that chimney with the aid of a roof ladder and with a safety harness; they would be quite safe up there and able to carry out any work that was required. But, I am over fifty as is 'A'. 'A' is also 6'3" and now weighs about 105 kilos. He didn't fancy it any more than I did.

Because the annexe was situated adjacent to the wall on which the fireplace was, it was impossible to erect a tower scaffold. The only other option was a cherry picker, and through my internet search I found out that we could hire one for 350 Euros a day. Given that we had never done this before we would probably need to hire it for two days. I ruled that out as an expensive option and the last resort.

Within two days, I had a response from the first wood burner installer with the professional Face book page. Well actually it was his girlfriend. She was very efficient and any misgivings I had soon dissolved. Five years earlier, I had read as many books about renovating a house in France that I could lay my hands on. After all, knowledge is power as the saying goes. In more than one book that I read, it said that ex- pat tradesmen were notoriously expensive and shoddy. They used their prime situation in the market place to full advantage. You see there are quite a few English people living in France, and many more with holiday homes. For years English people have been buying up run-down properties in France for a song. The French aren't interested in old houses and renovation like we are. They prefer to buy new. Very often, the people who buy these houses are 'more mature' and have very little by way of linguistic skills, and speak very little French. The idea of engaging a French tradesman fills them with dread because of the language barrier.

However, this email was quite comprehensive. I had stated in my email, that Vic, (the log burner installer) could go and visit my 'very dear friend' to look at the job, but I also sent some photos of the house and the fireplace. I received a prompt reply from the very efficient girlfriend and a quote, saying it was not necessary for Vic to visit. He was going to charge 1250 Euros which seemed quite steep to me, but that he was going to supply his own materials for fitting. I was told that this was because of insurance reasons in France and the work had to be certificated. He could only do that if he used his own guaranteed parts that he had supplied. When I considered that they would have to get on that roof and purchase the materials, the quote didn't look so bad. I sent all this advice to 'A'.

He had a bloody good whinge about it, and made me feel that it somehow I was partly to blame for the expensive quote. Vic could go and fit the wood burning stove on April 30th. 'A' sent me a message two days later asking me to instruct Vic to go ahead. Given the fact that 'A' had Vic's email address, and quite clearly was emailing me from the supermarket, I didn't understand why he hadn't just emailed Vic himself.

Over the course of the last few weeks waiting for the passport I had decided that it was quite impossible to travel out to France without my car. I had such a lot of things that I wanted to take with me, and the cost of sending them over separately was prohibitive compared with the ferry. It seemed sensible to take the car. I decided it was best not to tell 'A' about my decision and leave it as a *fait accompli.* He was already in a bad place and making nasty snide comments in his emails, and to such an extent that I was seriously considering calling the whole thing off. I already had enough on my plate and could do without the hassle.

Meanwhile, 'A' got on with trying to cut out the staggered breeze blocks that had been used to partially close the fire place opening. The fuss he made about that was incredible. He moaned about the noise from the angle grinder, and the dust. In fact he managed to burn out one angle grinder and had taken it back to the DIY store where they had replaced it for him. I was astounded as he admitted to using the blades 'till there was practically nothing left of them'. Then he attempted to render the inside of the fireplace with lime mortar and ended up with some in the crack of his arse, which had burned him rather badly. I know I shouldn't have, but I laughed when I read it. How the hell had he got it down the crack of his arse? I daren't ask. He said he hadn't realised that lime was such nasty stuff. This is a man who has a degree from Oxford and postgraduate qualifications.

I was supposed to arrive the day that Vic was due to install the wood burner, but my car had problems. I had booked to go on the early morning ferry from Plymouth, on the Tuesday morning after Easter Monday. When I got up on the Monday and went out to wash down my car, the back tyre was flat. This threw me into tailspin. Where the hell was I going to get a new tyre on a Bank holiday Monday? Nowhere was open. I didn't know what to do. I got my son to put the spare tyre on, but I wasn't happy with it. It was only when my father came back from his weekend away that he pointed out the sheer folly of my idea. "You can't go to France without a spare wheel," he said emphatically. He was of course right. He said he would pay. To say I was sailing close to the wind was putting it mildly. I had ten pounds left in my purse and the rest of my money was in the tank in the form of petrol, and even then it was touch and go whether it would be enough. My son said his girlfriend's uncle did tyre call out repairs, and he phoned him to come and have a look. But he wasn't going to arrive until 9pm because he had been away for the bank holiday too. Everything was going tits up. I was supposed to have an early night because I had to get up at 1am and set off for Plymouth.

I went to bed, but didn't sleep. I tossed and turned and then my son came in to me at 10am and said that the tyre was 'fucked' and the bloke didn't have one on his van. I had visions of being on the hard shoulder of the M5 in the middle of the night with a puncture and no spare tyre, with Clara and a juggernaut ploughing into us. It was not good. I decided to call the journey off. I would lose my money for the ferry booking as it was too late to cancel or re-schedule, but what was £140 compared to safety? The next time I would get some money was two weeks away, and I would go out then.

Chapter 12

The next morning I emailed 'A' to tell him that we would not be there as expected, and explained what had happened. I expected some acerbic response from him. I know it sounds as though he is a real dick, and I admit to a certain extent he is. If he had furnished me with enough money, then all of this wouldn't have been a problem but he was against me taking my car from the outset. To say we have a stormy relationship is putting it lightly. We have a long history, and he has issues with trust from his childhood. He should by rights, have gotten over them by the age of fifty one, but he hasn't. His heart attack and Brexit has only served to make him more bitter and untrusting and the last few weeks of being on his own had eroded what little optimism he had. He is also entirely lacking in self-discipline, something I find odd given that he likes to spend time on his own. I suspect this is out of his inability to get on with others for a sustained period of time, rather than a desire to be solitary. But I had embarked on a course of action and I was determined to see it through. It was too late to throw in the towel and call the whole thing off.

As it happened his email was okay. He was in *Carhaix* at the supermarket and Vic had arrived at the house with his assistant and he had left them to it. But things were not all good. Vic apparently had not got the necessary bits and pieces he said he was going to get to fit the log burner, so he was going to use 'A''s and would reduce the bill accordingly. I thought this was a positive.

But then the sting in the tail was, that Vic had not realised that 'A''s log burner had a back boiler and without this being hooked up to a central heating system, it meant that he couldn't use the log burner at all because having a fire would collapse the back boiler without water in it. The weather had turned cold again and 'A' was not very happy.

At least things were moving forward, if only slowly. The fireplace had been sorted and the log burner was in place. But 'A' was on a downer.

A couple of weeks earlier, 'A' had asked me to find an electrician as he wanted to get the house wired up properly. I was having difficulty finding someone and then I had a thought. During our email correspondence, I had struck up a rapport with Vic's girlfriend. So I emailed her and asked her if she knew of anyone. As luck would have it she did, and Tony was just starting up on his own. She gave me his email address. I emailed him and asked him to pop round and see 'A'.

'A' had told me that Tony had visited the house to look at what needed to be done, but despite asking 'A', it was only when I emailed Tony, that I knew he had actually given him a quote. I still didn't know whether 'A' had accepted. I didn't bother emailing Tony, as I didn't want to know that 'A' had not accepted, because he thought the price was too high. All 'A' had said in his emails was: "If it is under 2k Euros I will accept." I hoped sense would prevail, but I hadn't heard anything about it since that email.

The two weeks went by and 'A''s emails grew more and more worrying. He wasn't pleasant, and any attempts I made to chivvy him along fell on stony ground. He was severely depressed. I had deliberately avoided tempting fate by telling him the date I was going out there. I would turn up unannounced. The element of surprise would be the best approach I reasoned with myself.

On the Friday before I was due to depart the following Monday, I received a string of very nasty emails from him that almost had me giving up on the idea of going to France. It was clear he was in a bad place. It had been nearly two months since he had gone out to France. I would just have to summon every ounce of mental strength I had and get him out of his depression.

The weather was lovely and sunny, and the Monday morning of my departure it was glorious. I was booked on the 10pm ferry out of Plymouth that evening. I packed the car to the rafters trying not to forget anything for the trip. With an eight year old in tow, I had to make sure I had covered every eventuality. At least the weather was good, and I set off at 1pm on the Monday afternoon. I just hoped my twenty year old car would behave. In the past couple of months I had had to have the break line replaced and then I had to have a new tyre on because of a puncture. It was with trepidation that I travelled down the M5, constantly monitoring the cars temperature and petrol gauges for any sign that things might not be right.

We stopped at Taunton Dene services at 3.30pm to get a McDonalds Happy meal for Clara. I had plenty of snacks and drinks in the car, but as we wouldn't get on the ferry until 9pm at the earliest she needed something to eat before then. The sun was still shining and I was feeling more relaxed as we neared Plymouth.

We finally got to the port at about 5pm, and I phoned my son to let him know that we had arrived safely without event. He would tell my father. He is eighty and trying to have a telephone conversation with him is not easy. He is hard of hearing and as a general rule does not wear his hearing aid. He saves it for special occasions mainly because he says he can't be bothered to listen to the crap people talk.

Apart from a middle-aged couple with a touring caravan we were the first there. Lucky for them they had their caravan to chill in. We had to make do with the car. I was tempted to go into Plymouth, but then decided against it. We had arrived, and here we would stay until we boarded that ferry. Shit or bust I was going to France.

It was a long wait for me, but an interminable one for an eight year old, and we tried to pass the time with a game of eye spy and trying to empty the car of any rubbish we had accumulated over the course of the journey; interspersed with trips to the public toilets on the quayside. Finally at about 8pm we were allowed through passport control to the front of the quay.

It had taken a couple of hours and a lot of skill to pack that car. The lawnmower was on the front passenger seat of the car and in the foot well was my computer in a bag with notebooks and some practice maths books for my daughter. I had also managed to stuff a bag of clothes and a pillow in there as well. On the back seat next to Clara, was a small TV, a DVD, a double duvet, another bag of clothes and another pillow. In the boot of the car, I had packed a boot jack, two pair of wellies (one for me and one for Clara), a bag of shoes, a cagoule, a fleece, three Le Creuset saucepans, a stock pot, a casserole dish, two months supply of teabags (4 per day x 7 = 28 x 8 =224 +51 spare = 275), kitchen utensils and some kitchen knives, two trowels, a lump hammer , bolster and stone chisel, a box of vegetable seeds, my wax pot (for waxing my legs), hair dye, peroxide and mixing dishes, towels, a blanket, a box of Lego and my most prized possession, my sun lounger. All of this in a convertible! Just think what I could have taken if I had an estate.

We had to pass through a hangar where customs officials were waiting. The window was already down on my door as the weather was very warm. "Is this your car?" asked the customs official.

"Yes," I replied.

"Did you pack it yourself?"

"Yes, I did," I replied rather smugly. There wasn't an inch of spare space in that car.

"Have you got any petrol or anything flammable in the car? He asked. I immediately thought of the lawn mower on the front passenger seat.

"I emptied the lawnmower of petrol," I replied, again feeling rather proud of myself for doing that.

"I will check that in a minute." said the customs official. "Have you got anything that could be construed as a dangerous weapon?" he asked.

Now that was a tricky one. I had some kitchen knives in the boot and some peroxide which they wouldn't allow on aircraft, but I felt confident that these were for domestic purposes, so I said. "No." Hoping he wouldn't look.

"Can you pop the bonnet for me?" he said. I thought it odd that he wanted to look at the engine but what the hell, if that is what he wanted, and then I would oblige and pulled the bonnet lever. He stood by the bonnet waiting. I assumed that he didn't know where the catch was as it is rather hidden on my car. But he just stood there looking.

"Can't you find the bonnet catch?" I enquired poking my head out of the window.

"I wanted you to do it so that I would know if this was your car." He replied.

"Oh," I said and laughed and got out of the car and lifted the bonnet for him.

Then he asked to look in the boot. A female customs official had joined him. I lifted the boot lid. It was crammed. He looked in at the boot and I prayed that he didn't want me to empty it. It would take me ages to get it back in. Thankfully the silence was broken by the woman "And that is how a woman packs a car," she said and laughed. Thankfully he was satisfied that I wasn't a terrorist. I mean what kind of sick individual takes a lawnmower, an eight year old child and a stuffed toy guinea pig called Gary on a terrorist mission?

We were waved through to the front of quayside where we had a bird's eye view of the sea and the approaching ferry when it did turn up. I looked across at the car next to us. There were two old ladies in a small car waiting to board the ferry. They had all sorts of domestic goods piled high on their back seat. How wonderful for them, I thought to myself. They must have a holiday home somewhere. But it is still brave of them to go on a ferry and drive to France. That takes a certain amount of grit at their age.

Chapter 13

Eventually the ferry came into view. Was I relieved? I wanted a glass of wine and something to eat. It was dusk when we boarded the ferry and parked up. We immediately went to the cafe and grabbed a bite to eat. I had never been on the Plymouth to Roscoff ferry before and it was smaller than the large one used on the Portsmouth to St Malo crossing but it looked newer. It was more or less the same set up and we chose the self service restaurant option. I had a tuna *niçoise* salad and a half bottle of wine. I was in need of two glasses of wine I had decided because I was sleeping on the floor that night.

We made up our bed on the floor of the lounge where our seats were allocated. I had taken a duvet to lie on, a couple of pillows and a blanket to cover us. I would sleep fully clothed, but my daughter put on her pyjamas. There were not many other people in the lounge, probably about half a dozen at the most, mainly men on their own, some of whom I suspected were truck drivers. There was one bohemian type bloke, like myself who had got his sleeping bag on the floor. The others sat in the reclining chairs looking most uncomfortable. I did notice one man move onto the floor from his chair halfway through the night obviously realising that it was the better option, despite being hard.

The wine, tiredness and the sound of the engine of the boat soon lulled us to sleep. I do love my creature comforts and despite having a pocket sprung mattress together with a feather topper on my bed at home I didn't mind the floor of the lounge for one night, in fact I think it is preferable to the windowless cabins with bunk beds. If I had money, I would of course pay for one of the deluxe cabins with portholes. You never know, one day in the future I may be able to afford one, but I am not holding my breath.

The lovely thing about sleeping on the lounge floor is that you are woken by the dawn creeping up over the horizon. The dark slowly giving way to the light that heralds a new day. I was excited about my little adventure. I was going to work like a dog to move that project forward, even if it would take all my skills of diplomacy and self restraint.

The ferry docked promptly and we were ready to depart. I had breakfast snack type things with us, and drink so I avoided the expense of an unpleasant cup of take-away tea. Unlike the journey from St Malo, I hadn't travelled this road before and it is no good asking an eight year old to map read. I had made a list of the road numbers we had to take and felt confident that it would be okay.

It was a beautiful morning and although it had been five years since I had been in France it soon came back to me just how lovely the French countryside is. We passed fields of globe artichokes, something we don't see in England. I don't think we know what to do with them and I have only ever seen them for sale in Waitrose. Obviously the French adore, them judging by the field after field of them I passed.

But then somewhere near *Morlaix* I got lost. I must have missed the turning. Instead of turning around, I took a road to *Morlaix,* confident that I would be able to pick up the trail to *Carhaix* somewhere. How wrong I was. I stopped to look at the Michelin map in a wooded lay by, on the way into *Morlaix* and I couldn't even find what road I was on. We drove into *Morlaix* which is situated on the mouth of the estuary; the road in ran along one side of the quay and the road out ran along the other. The houses were painted pretty pastel shades and boats lined the quayside. *Morlaix* itself is nestled between two cliffs. I finally saw a road sign for *Carhaix* at the end of town and took the turning only to find that the road was closed for road works.

I turned around on a car park and went back to where I had turned off and took the next turning. Perhaps I could pick up the road to *Carhaix* further on. I drove deeper and deeper into countryside and was certain I was now on a minor road. I didn't come across a single road sign and decided that I was well and truly lost. The next village I came too I would stop and ask for help. It hadn't gone long when I did indeed come upon a little village. It had a local shop, a hairdresser, estate agents and a *tabac*. After debating with myself, I decided to try the *tabac*. I could see the hairdresser sitting behind her reception desk with not a customer in sight, but I doubted her English would be good enough and my French too poor for us to communicate. We got out of the car and went into the dimly lit interior of the *tabac*. I don't know why, but I have been in several *tabacs* in rural France and they all have the same feel to them. The interiors are dark and very 'manly' in their decor. Men, usually elderly ones sit on bar chairs at the bar chatting away about God knows what. I suppose it is the equivalent of the local pub in England, but *tabacs* are open at 7am in the morning. Rarely have I seen a woman in a *tabac*.

There was a swarthy looking bartender aged about forty behind the bar with a tea towel slung over his left shoulder. I approached the barman and said *"Parlais vous Anglais? Je suis perdu;"* which was about all I could muster in French at the time, even though I had been practising for months on the Duolingo app on my phone and had considered myself pretty good. Another little phrase I had got ready in advance was *"Je suis desole, ma francais c'est nes pas bien;"* which means to those of you who don't speak a word of French; "I'm sorry but my French is not good." I thought this would come in handy if anyone started babbling on in French thinking I was fluent, which I most certainly was not.

The bartender replied yes much to my relief, and I told him that I was looking for *Carhaix Plouguer* and could he give me directions. He looked at me as though I was asking to be directed to Paris and I had the sinking feeling that I had gone way off course. If that was the case, I was in great danger of running out of petrol before I got to *Carhaix*. He said that he didn't know how to get there, but the man at the far end of the bar would. We both walked over to the barman while the locals were talking about me in French. I knew they were talking about me, although what they were saying I had no idea. The man at the end of the bar couldn't speak English, so the barman translated and was even kind enough to give me a pen and paper so that I could write the directions down. I was very relieved and I thanked them all profusely as I left. I must have been the highlight of their morning and they would no doubt be talking about me for a good while after I had left, as I got the distinct impression that nothing much happened in that village.

The directions proved to be spot on, and in no time at all I was back on track. It was now 10am in the morning. A journey that should have taken 50 minutes had taken over an hour and a half. We finally pulled up outside the house at 10.30am. It was clear that 'A' was still in bed as there was no sign of life. The outside of the house looked abandoned. The shutters downstairs were still fastened shut, and ivy had taken hold on the stonework on the house. The steps leading up to the front door were nearly covered in it. The undergrowth surrounding the house was very overgrown and the meadow opposite had turned into a jungle.

Chapter 14

It had been nearly five years since I had visited the house and it had been autumn then, now it was May. I stood and looked at the house and its surrounds. It was still beautiful even in its neglected state. How could anyone not love it here? I thought to myself.

There was still no sign of life from the house, yet the upstairs window was open and surely 'A' must have heard us. He clearly hadn't been doing any work in the previous two months he had been here. I told Clara to go and knock on the door. He would have heard our voices even if he had been asleep. It took a while, but he opened the door. I was right about the element of surprise, because he looked very shocked.

"Hello," I said cheerily.

"I thought you were the electrician," he said. "Tony said he wasn't coming today so I had a lie in." Well at least the electrician was actually wiring the house. He must have accepted his quote. I put the kettle on and surveyed the room. It was a tip. Plasterboards were lent against the wall obscuring the window. Boxes of kitchen equipment lay unpacked and dusty. Tools and machinery lay strewn across the floor. I had arrived in the nick of time. I made a coffee for 'A' and a tea for me. I put his mug in front of him. He still looked shocked.

"I didn't expect you to come at all," he said with his head in his hands. "I don't know why you have come. It is not a suitable environment for a child. It is a building site. It is not safe," he added, probably regretting his vile emails the week before.

"I have come to help," I said, "and Clara is not three anymore, she is eight. It will be okay. But if you don't want us here, we can go." I said, not meaning it really.

He sat silent for a while. "I am sure that in a couple of days I will be glad you have come, but it is just a shock that is all." He said still not looking at me.

I had to redeem the situation. "You have done a good job on that fireplace," I said admiring his rendering.

"It is a shame I can't use it. Bloody Vic what's his face." He said angrily.

"When is he coming back to do the plumbing and rig up the back boiler?" I asked innocently. It was a fair enough question and a logical step.

"I am not having that crook back here," he said emphatically.

Oh dear, I thought to myself. He really was in a bad place. "At least he used your flue and the other bits that you bought." I said on a more positive note, but it didn't make any difference.

Later, when the caffeine from his coffee had kicked in and he had got over the shock, he was a little more positive. Admittedly, I had praised all his efforts with the plaster boarding and said that I had underestimated just how much had done five years ago. I persuaded him to open the shutters downstairs to let light into the room, and he admitted that he had kept them closed to stop the neighbours looking in. He had been avoiding Pascal and Michelle like the plague, staying upstairs and keeping the door closed in the hope that they would leave him alone.

"I think they are pissed off with me," he said. I could see why that might be, but said nothing. I think I would be pretty pissed off with some foreigner who had bought a house nearby, who had not visited or done anything to renovate it in five years and then when he did turn up, still did nothing. However, that was all going to be rectified now that I had arrived.

He decided that we should go into *Carhaix* in his van to get some shopping supplies and a mattress for Clara's bed. He gave me 100 Euros for housekeeping for a week and said that he wouldn't give me anymore if I ran out. I don't know why he feels like he has to be a dick about things, perhaps it asserts his manhood to do it? But I am quite used to managing on a shoestring, and it would be no problem for me to budget. We climbed into the van. I sat in the back on a couple of old coats as promised. I think he thought that it was some sort of humiliation and punishment for me to ride in the back of a van, but then he doesn't really know me that well. He has always had a chip on shoulder about my father having 'money'. It is not that my father is rich, by any stretch of the imagination; he has worked very hard all his life and had his own construction company. But 'A' has a 'thing' about people who have money, even if they have worked for it, something he seems to overlook. He could have had money, if he had stuck out his job as a senior prosecutor working for the Crown Prosecution Service. Instead he prefers to bum about teaching English as a foreign language for peanuts, and then have a couple of years off until things get difficult and he is forced back to work.

So I was quite happy in the back of the van. The sun was shining I was in France and about to visit a French supermarket. What more could a girl want?

Carhaix is about 8 miles away from *Cleden Poher*. It is a quaint town with a main street running through it. *Tabacs*, bars, a couple of *patisserie/boulangerie* places and a *charcuterie* all feature along the main street together with some hairdressers, beauticians, travel agents and posh looking shops selling clothes and shoes. At the top end of the town, there is a square by the town hall with restaurants and more bars, a fishmongers and a launderette. Further down the main street, is the market place with public toilets that I would become intimately acquainted with over the next few weeks. There is also a curious sculpture. It is three bronze figures of old Breton women in traditional costume. I have to say that they are rather ugly and a little bit scary. A market is held on this car park once a week on a Saturday.

Surrounding *Carhaix* is a ring road. Here is where the major shops are situated. There are five supermarkets in *Carhaix* on the outskirts of town. A Lidl and Le Clerc sit at the bottom end of the town. There is a Netto on the ring road and there is an Intermarche at the top end of the town by the hospital. There is a Casino supermarket near the public car park, but it is small and I have never been in there. I would say it is like a convenience supermarket pretty much like our Tesco Express here in England.

Before we visited a supermarket however we needed to purchase a single mattress for Clara's bed. For this we went to a shop called 'IF' (well I think that is what it was called but I might have got that wrong, perhaps it was 'Go'. I do remember it being a rather odd name for a shop.) This was a small home goods store. They sold bits of furniture – not a lot, just basic items and white goods. But they did sell mattresses and we were in luck. The cheapest they had was 50 Euros. It was only foam and not wonderful but Clara is only eight and there was no point in buying anything better because we wouldn't be here for months on end, and the mouse problem would return and they would probably nibble at the mattress. At least the price tag met 'A''s approval, so we took it to the till and paid for it, then loaded it in the back of the van. My seating arrangement in the van had now got a lot more comfortable thanks to the mattress.

'A''s spirits were picking up, I was pleased to note, even though he had just parted with 50 Euros. We drove around to Le Clerc. 'A' had said he preferred Le Clerc to Intermarche as it was cheaper. I took him on his word. I don't think it really is any cheaper to be honest, but there was a cafe at Le Clerc where 'A' could purchase a cafe au lait for one euro and sit for two hours using their free wifi. When I had been in France five years earlier, the Lidl had been closed for refurbishing and I had used the Intermarche as they had washing machines outside, on the car park which I used whilst I shopped.

In France, a large area of the car parks in the bigger supermarkets like Intermarche and Le Clerc are covered. Isn't that just wonderful? It means that if it is pissing it down, you can park undercover and keep dry and in the summer if it is baking hot, your car will be kept cool. They also have a covered area where they generally have a couple of washing machines, (one for a larger load, one for a normal load) and a tumble drier. In 2019 it cost four Euros for a load of washing in the normal machine and eight Euros for a large. The drier started at twenty cents for about five minutes. 'A' told me, that the price includes washing powder (you have to pay extra for fabric softener) but to be honest it is the environmentally friendly stuff and with 'A' working on the house getting rather dirty, I started to add some of my own to the wash as the clothes never smelled very fresh if I just relied on the included washing detergent. You can pay by card or coin for the washers and driers, and they conveniently told you via a digital display how long it would be until the cycle finished, so you could make a note of it and go and do your shopping then come back.

I left 'A' and Clara in the coffee shop and went to browse Le Clerc. If I was to budget I needed to recce the prices. Le Clerc is pretty much like any large supermarket back home such as Tesco, Sainsbury's etc., in that it sells an array of goods such as stationery, a few garden supplies, a few toys, some car essentials like engine oil and jump leads, household cleaning goods. It also has a bakery/cake section, a meat counter, a deli counter and a fish counter. I wandered the aisles and marvelled at the goods for sale. The bakery section sold different kinds of breads from the traditional baguettes to sliced bread, brioche, buns and pitta bread. The cakes on offer were just out of this world. Fruit flans, gateaux, rum babas, huge chocolate éclairs and other delectable treats. I stood there and looked at the array on offer for several minutes. But they are not cheap.

The meat I noticed was pricey. More expensive than at home, but they sold just about every cut imaginable including offal. We tend to be a bit squeamish about eating offal in Britain, but they don't seem to feel the same in France, if the meat counter was anything to go by.

On the deli counter there were all sorts of things to buy. A little like Tesco's here where you can buy rotisserie chickens and sausage rings, you could buy cooked chickens and ham hocks in Le Clerc. You could also buy potato gratin and other hot vegetable accompaniments so that you could purchase an entire meal ready cooked to take home. They also sold salads, salami's, ham, quiche and black pudding and cheese. OMG Cheese! There was an entire aisle in the supermarket devoted to cheese alone.

The fish counter was impressive. I mean seriously impressive. They had a tank full of live crabs and lobsters, and on the counter itself there was just about every type of seafood imaginable; cockles, mussels, oysters, clams, shrimps, prawns and langoustines. They had a pretty good array of fish too. It made the fish counter at my local Morrison's look pathetic.

I was in absolute heaven in that supermarket, but I realised that my 100 Euros housekeeping was not going to stretch very far if I did my weekly shop in Le Clerc. I needed to go and look in Lidl.

I went back to 'A' and Clara sitting in the coffee shop. Thankfully, he still had a lot of downloading to do so I was free to go to Lidl. He said to take the van as he had insured me to drive it. My car is an automatic as I suffer from arthritis in my left knee and not having to use a clutch makes life tolerable. It had been a while since I had drove a manual, let alone a van but thankfully it was fairly easy to drive and I soon got the hang of it. I only had to drive about

500 yards to Lidl. They do not have a covered car park but I suppose it is a budget supermarket. I was careful and parked miles away from other cars.

Lidl in France is pretty much like Lidl in the UK apart from the goods on offer. I did notice some things that are the same. Their special buys for a start off are generally very similar, apart from the one week they were selling pool cleaner on a special buy. Obviously more French people have swimming pools than we do, as I have never seen pool cleaner on special buy here.

Their bakery section however was covered and you had to use a mechanical arm to select your bread roll or pastry and push it to the centre chute from where you could collect it and put it into a bag. It was in Lidl that I discovered *chouquettes*. *Chouquettes* are little mouthfuls of choux pastry, (much like an unfilled profiterole) with sugar crystals dotted on the outside. Lidl sell them for eight cents a time (about 5p) so you can have a bag of ten for the equivalent of 50p and my goodness, they are fantastic. A baguette was 40 cents in Lidl compare to 80 cents in Le Clerc. It would be Lidl where I would be doing the bulk of my shop each week I decided.

I went back to 'A' and told him all about Lidl. He agreed to come with me when he had finished downloading, as I needed him to choose some wine for us to drink.

Chapter 15

After Lidl we headed back to the house. It was still lovely and sunny and I felt sure that I would enjoy my stay in France. I had taken four jars of curry sauce out to France with me and I was going to cook a curry that evening as Indian food is a particular favourite of 'A''s and Clara loves it too. 'A' explained that you can buy curry sauce in the supermarket, but it is expensive. In fact, as I was to discover, they have an aisle with certain foods for ex-pats such as HP brown sauce, salad cream and curry sauces. I can't understand why with the cornucopia of wonderful foods on offer in a French supermarket how anyone would get homesick for such stuff, but I suppose ex-pats hanker for things they can no longer have. Mine was a good strong teabag, but I had come equipped.

That evening, after eating, I made the bed up for Clara with bedding I had brought with me from England. I was thankful that I had decided to take my car packed to the rafters, as they were things that I had spare, that we needed over in France. I had brought a change of bedclothes for 'A''s bed which was just as well, as his were filthy. His bottom sheet was no longer white as it had once been. God only knew how often he changed his bedding, and given that I would be sharing a bed with him I changed them. I shuddered when I looked at that filthy sheet. It would need boiling to get it white again.

After watching a family friendly film on 'A''s laptop we went to bed. The windows were open upstairs and after Clara had fallen asleep I stood at the window looking out onto the meadow. It was very overgrown, and I would start tackling it straight away in the morning. I would first mow the verge outside of the house, as that is where we parked the cars. The grass was nearly a foot tall.

I had to share a bed with 'A' as there was nowhere else to sleep, but it wasn't going to be a problem as any form of intimacy between us had been a no go zone since he had had his heart attack. We were just simply 'friends'.

Much to my surprise, 'A' woke at around 3.30am and asked if I was awake. I usually wake up in the early hours, especially in the summer, as I tend to do my writing early in the morning. I find the quiet helps me tremendously, as well as having no interruptions. It was very quiet here in rural France. There was no sound at all and it was pitch black. 'A' had left a lamp on downstairs the night before, because there were no banisters on the hole in the floor where the stairs came up. He went and made a drink for us both. We sat in the candle light from a hurricane lamp I had brought with me and chatted. It was clear he had much on his mind and was very depressed.

"I wished I had never bought this place," he said.

My heart sank. I had my work cut out trying to get him in a happy place. "How can you say that?" I said, "It is so beautiful here. If you hadn't have bought this place you would have spent the money by now and have nothing to show for it."

He blamed Brexit, and his heart attack. It was no good trying to make him see sense. He was on a major downer and would not be talked out of it. I pointed out that he would find it difficult to sell at the moment and not just because of Brexit. He had started to renovate and the majority of people would not want to buy a half finished house. They would have to live with his chosen layout. The French wouldn't touch it, and the English would be wary about buying given the uncertainty over Brexit. He might be able to sell it, but he would it would be at a knock down price. I despaired to be honest, but I have known him for many years and it was no good trying to get him to change his outlook, I just hoped that he would change his mind over the next few weeks.

Tony the electrician was returning that day to continue working on the house. 'A' didn't want to be in while he worked, so he said we would go into *Carhaix*. "He is pissing me off to be honest," he said, "I asked him to put the junction box over the French windows and it looks like he is putting it in here." he said.

"Well you will just have to tell him," I said. What was wrong with the man? I wasn't sure if it was nit-picking or whether he hated parting with his hard-earned cash. I say hard-earned, but I am not sure that teaching counts as hard work. It wasn't like it was hard physical labour, and as he was abroad he didn't have the tax man taking a large percentage of his salary.

So, after breakfast Tony arrived at about 9am and 'A' had a chat with him, and then we went into *Carhaix* again. 'A' said he needed some washing doing and he would treat Clara to a McDonalds.

I spent a good deal of time during those first few weeks acting as a shoulder to cry on for 'A'. He says he likes his solitude, but really it is because he has difficulty with personal relationships. They start off okay, but when they encounter difficulties it all goes tits up, he takes umbrage over something and decides not to have anything to do with that person again. I am only still his friend because we have a daughter together. If it hadn't been for that I would probably have cut him off years ago. But over time I have learned to deal with him but even now, he gets to me sometimes and makes me very angry.

We visited Netto at my request. Netto in *Carhaix* is small with a limited array of goods but it is cheap. I purchased a five gallon container of water, as the water container that 'A' was using had algae in it. It was okay for washing up, but not for drinking. I could also re-use the container to fill from the stop tap for future drinking water. I hadn't commented on the algae ridden water container, as 'A' would see it as criticism. I am normally a very forthright person. I am honest to the point of being blunt, and I don't suffer fools gladly. But I am aware that this can be rather offensive, and I only tend to do it with people I know very well. It was going to take every ounce of self control to not be critical of 'A'. I was trying to get him out of his depressed state, not send him hurtling deeper into it, but it was very wearing to be honest.

Netto was cheap and cheerful, and they sold a limited array of vegetables at cheap prices. I purchased a few items. My housekeeping was going down rapidly. The problem was that 'A' didn't really cook as such, and he had few of the household store cupboard items that I needed for cooking a meal. Things such as olive oil, stock cubes, tomato puree, herbs, onions, garlic, potatoes, rice and other essentials such as toilet roll. Up until now he had been using paper napkins he had 'obtained' from McDonalds on his weekly visits. We ladies needed toilet rolls. As we were only going to go shopping twice a week, we also need bread. The *boulangerie* in *Cleden Poher*, had closed in the five years that I had not been there, but I discovered those vacuum packed part-baked baguettes were the perfect solution, so I bulk bought. After a couple of weeks, things would even out I was sure as I got used to the supermarkets, their prices and what was cheaper and where. Unless you are rich, as most of us are not, you get to know what is cheaper at which supermarket. Shopping has become a nightmare these days and it is no different in France. But I was sorely missing the pound shop.

Something I ought to mention about shopping in France is that most shops shut from 12 – 2pm for lunch. It had come as something of a revelation five years earlier whilst operating on 'A''s timetable. This meant that he lazed about in bed until 10am and then got up. By the time we hit the shops it was about 11am. I remember one time we visited a DIY shop only to find it was shut. It is the same with Builders merchants and other non grocery shops. Le Clerc stays open because it has a cafe which is absolutely rammed at lunch time with people eating a three course lunch. This is amazing to us Brits. Lunch is the main meal of the day for the French and that is why they take two hours over it. Restaurants are busy at lunchtime in rural France but on an evening everything is closed by 9pm. The previous time we had visited France all those years ago and stayed in the caravan, we had decided the one evening that we were having such a good time we needed another bottle of wine.

The village *tabac* was shut and it was only 8.30pm so we had to drive into *Carhaix*. We passed bars that were closed on the way into town and arriving in the main street everything was dead. What did the French do on an evening? More to the point what did the young French people do on an evening in rural France? We found a bar open and I bravely went in, fortified by wine it has to be said and in pigeon French, I asked the bartender for a bottle of wine. He looked at me like I had landed from Mars. Luckily, there were some young men playing pool and understanding my predicament, one of them came to my rescue and told me that the kebab shop across the street sold wine by the bottle to take-out.

Feeling rather shame-faced about my seemingly obvious desperate alcoholism, I went into the kebab shop and ordered a kebab and casually asked for a bottle of wine. I ordered the kebab as a cover for the real reason I was there, which was the wine. When I returned to the car, 'A' asked why I had bought a kebab. When I told him, he laughed heartily, but he thanked me later because he ate that kebab and pronounced it 'gourmet'. On hearing this I had a sample myself and I can honestly say that it was the best kebab I had ever eaten from such a shop. My previous experience of a kebab was after a drunken evening in Oxford from a roadside trailer that had ended in food poisoning the next day which had put me off take-away kebabs for years afterwards.

But I digress. We had done our shopping and were off to McDonalds. Now I am no fan of that fast food chain at all. I understand the appeal for small people and large men. Food you don't have to cook for large men and a toy that accompanies a meal for a small child. But Macki D's in France is in an altogether different league to the ones in England. The toys that accompany the meal are nicer, and are actually something worth having. During the two months we were there, they offered story books and Mr Men Toys. The meal is different too. Not only do you get chicken nuggets or a burger (or a *croque monsieur* – cheese and ham toastie to you and I), you have the option of french fries, cucumber slices, carrot batons, or fruit slices and you get a desert! Your child can choose from a yoghurt, fruit or an ice cream and the concept of eating in is rather more elegant than that of eating at home.

After the McDonalds 'Francais' experience we went back to the house.

Chapter 16

'A' was dismayed that it was still only early afternoon and Tony would still be working. I couldn't understand his problem with this and told him so. "The thing is Joanne, is that the house is a shit hole and I am embarrassed about it."

I couldn't believe my ears. "'A', this is not new to tradesmen. They are used to people living in half-finished houses that resemble building sites."

He seemed to find little comfort in this. "Yes, but we have no running water and no toilet." He added. Point taken.

Normally the first job you would do is to have your septic tank installed, but with Le Stêr that, was not possible. It sat on a flood plain and I had translated the septic tank report years earlier. Because of the flood plain, the filtration bed would have to be sited along the lane, which would be higher than the tank that received the raw sewage and therefore needed a pump to pump the effluent up to the filtration bed. This meant that it could not be used intermittently. Someone would have to be in residence permanently to make sure the electric pump was working and was fed with enough shit to keep it working, which is why the locals had turned down the offer to purchase the property. It would not make a suitable '*Gite*'.

So the house had to be renovated first and the septic tank was the last thing that had to be done when someone was ready to live there full time.

Any way, we went back to the house. I was eager to start work on chopping back that undergrowth. It wasn't that hot and it was still tolerable to work. We arrived back at the house and I filled the mower with petrol. Because of the lack of a shower, and washing machine I put on my dungarees that my middle daughter had bought for me at my request for my birthday. I also took the added precaution of putting a bandana on my hair. The sun was shining and I was prepared to fire up that beast when along came 'A''s neighbour Pascal on his bicycle, on his way to the trash at the end of the road.

Sorry but I have to explain about the trash. In rural France we didn't have a rubbish bin outside of our house. It was a large 'Biffa bin' at the end of the lane where we deposited our household waste in bin bags to be collected once a week. We shared this facility with *Le Manor* and the lock-keepers cottage. There was also a cage into which we deposited recyclable stuff such as plastic, cardboard and cans in yellow recycling bags that we obtained from the *Mairie's* office. The glass bottle recycling centres, for some unfathomable reason that I could not ascertain, but guessed at, were out of town by the roadside. They are conveniently placed, so you could stop your car on the way into town and dispose of the evidence of your large alcohol consumption in relative privacy. The French obviously like their wine to such an extent that they don't want you to feel guilty about it; how thoughtful.

So Pascal stopped on his way to recycle. From the back of his house, he has a clear view of *Le Stêr* across the meadow. He is retired. We (or at least 'A') are something of an oddity, and he had clearly noticed the arrival of my car the day before. Although we had been out most of the time yesterday and today, now we were in and outside as well. He must have wasted no time in collecting what little they had by way of recycling and getting on his bike to take it to the trash. Any normal person would have waited until they were going into town and loaded it in the boot of their car, to stop off on the way, but he wanted an excuse to stop by.

"*Bonjour*," he said as I bent over the mower. 'A' was stood on the steps. I knew there was some sarcastic remark coming.

"*Bonjour Pascal*," I said and we exchanged the *ça va, ça va* routine.

Then he said, "What has happened 'A'?" Aah there it was I thought to myself.

But 'A' rose to the bait. "What do you mean Pascal?" he said innocently, and there Pascal had him.

"Why are you working?" he said triumphantly.

So I headed him off at the pass and said, "*Madame arrivè*". He laughed and had nothing more to say. I had been rehearsing that moment for weeks. We watched as he cycled up the lane with a very empty yellow recycling bag.

"Well you put him in his place," said 'A' and laughed.

"I told you he would be over as soon as he clocked my car," I said. "You worry too much. He has nothing better to do. He is retired and bored shitless. You and I are his only form of entertainment beyond wine and television." I tugged on the pull cord on the mower and it whirred into life.

It is one of those hardy petrol mowers with a Briggs and Stratton engine and a rotary blade and will cut through almost anything. You can raise the wheels to enable it to cut rough tall grass and lower them to get a finer cut. It won't do bowling green stripes however, but that is fine because I wanted to mow 12 inch grass on a verge at the moment. Within half an hour the verges were looking rather good. A was so inspired he took it a step further and started cutting into the long grass on the meadow. I had not seen him this enthused for ages.

We had a jolly couple of hours before the mower kept cutting out. 'A' was working it too hard. There were brambles in the meadow where he had attempted to cut and it would need a heavy weight strimmer. It had been left for five years and the result was a jungle. We decided to call it quits for the day and crack open the wine.

Oh the wine. Well, it is France. Three Euros a bottle and it is good. You don't get a headache in the morning. We tried various price ranges (although not top end, as we couldn't afford it) and I have to say that cheap and cheerful was the best for us. We have no palate you see. Years of drinking supermarket plonk in England put us firmly in the novice category when it came to wine consumption. I don't want a sophisticated bouquet of brambles and spice, I want something that gets me pissed, doesn't taste like paint stripper and doesn't give me a hangover, and French wine doesn't do that. I have concluded that unless you spend £15 quid plus on a bottle of French wine in England, then you shouldn't bother as the French send all of their crap over to us, and at an inflated price. Like anyone with any sense, they save the best for themselves; how utterly sensible.

Tony left for the day. He had done quite a lot. And, he had moved the junction box. The sun was shining, 'A' was in a good mood and all was well with the world. So far I was having a good time and I started to prepare dinner.

Now it wasn't the easiest of things to do in the house; cook dinner. There was the lack of available work surfaces and the lack of running water, but I was managing to do a pretty good job. With the kitchen stuff I had taken out with me I was coping quite well. I had my prized set of *le creuset* saucepans that my late brother had given me a couple of years earlier ,when he had had a clear out. I loved my brother, but he was a sucker for a Homes and Gardens magazine and he had a barn conversion and an Aga, hence the le creuset saucepans in the classic red. I think he had long since got pissed off with them, which is why they had lain in a cupboard for years until he had a clear out and given them to me. But now at last they were in their rightful home in France. I can see why. They are very heavy and if you live in rural France a burglar is not a common occurrence, so you have no need for any security system. Why would you when you have a set of *le crueset* saucepans? One of those is so heavy (even the milk pan) that if you don't get a sprained wrist from using them, one blow from a *le creuset* saucepan would render any intruder senseless if not dead.

We had a lovely meal, and I washed up in the Belfast sink that was raised on breeze blocks with a bucket under the waste, which I had to throw on the meadow after every washing up session.

As I washed up and then replenished the water supply (no easy task, as I had to go outside, lift a concrete slab, put the hose in the container and turn it on, all at stooping level). The lack of running water was a real pain in the arse. I was beginning to understand how life must have been hundreds of years ago for people, when they had to go outside and use a well, or if they were really posh a pump. But for someone living in this day and age it was just a pain in the arse. It took so much time. You take it for granted to turn on a tap and have running water. I was spending so much of my time doing the essentials, such as refilling water containers, heating water in saucepans to wash up or wash hands or anything else; it was like camping, only this was no holiday and there was work to be done and the more time I wasted on this shit the less time I would work.

We needed to get running water into the house and fast. I vowed to speak with 'A'. Thankfully it was spring and hunting season was finished for a couple of months, and I had heard no trace of the hunting dogs. Perhaps they were being fed regularly?

Chapter 16

It was another night of going to sleep early. Not as though it bothered me. I was knackered. We all sat in bed and watched a family friendly film on 'A''s computer courtesy of pirate bay and then by the time I had lain by Clara I had fallen asleep myself. I awoke an hour later and crawled into bed with 'A' who was asleep; poor love. We had disturbed his routine. He was not used to living with other people. He operated by night, and slept in the day and we had turned his routine completely on its head. Although it did have compensations, I cooked his meals and washed up. I also shopped and did the washing; and he had company.

He woke early the next morning at about 4am. I think I realised after a few days that he relished these moments; moments when we could talk quietly, without being interrupted with mundane tasks, or Clara demanding either my or his attention. It was a time when we could both sit silently at times thinking and then we could talk. I must confess that I enjoyed these moments too. I shall always remember them fondly.

He lit the candle in the hurricane lamp and went and made a drink. I sensed he had something on his mind. He came back and handed me my drink. Then he talked about his past, about his mother, about his heart attack, about Brexit and about his dreams crumbling into dust. My heart went out to him. He just didn't see the world as I see it. I see everything as a challenge; an obstacle is something to get over. You just have to find a way; after all, nothing in life worth having is ever easy, right? But not to 'A', he saw life as one long struggle, one long battle and everything went tits up. Well it is going to if you have that outlook on life.

I had to tread carefully. I listened and said nothing and just when I thought I could take no more he lay down and slept. I guess he had blown himself out with all that self-pity, just as the sun rose above the horizon and illuminated the room. I lay there wide awake, watching the dawn on a lovely spring morning, listening to the birds sing such a wonderful song. Apart from the birds, nothing else could be heard above his breathing. I know he had suffered a major setback with his heart attack, but he was still alive and he owned this place. It was truly breathtakingly beautiful. How could he not be in love with it? I was. No matter the lack of sanitation, no matter the lack of running water. But soon it would have electricity. It would have lights and plug sockets. So what if the log burner wasn't working yet? It would be and soon if I had anything to do with it. *Le Stêr* would have running water. He had done so much partitioning upstairs and so much plaster boarding, it was, to my reckoning a third of the way there. He couldn't give up now.

Unable, and not wanting to go back to sleep, I lay and thought and listened to the birds and watched the sky through the open window. If you have ever lived in a conurbation like I have spent most of my life, you will appreciate the view I had. It was not one of other people's houses and there were no street lights to obscure my view. All I saw were trees and skyline and there was no sound apart from the birds chirruping. No cars, no buzz of electricity cables, no background noise. It was absolutely perfect. How could he not want this? I vowed to be patient with him; he needed to be made to appreciate what he had.

7am came quickly and I decided to get up. Although I couldn't have a shower, I could have a strip wash. I put the water on to boil in a saucepan and got my face flannel, soap and towel ready. It was much colder downstairs than up, but that didn't deter me. He may have been living like a hog since he had arrived, but I was a woman and I was going to bring civilisation to this house if it was the last thing I did.

I worked quickly stripping down and using the hot water, flannel and soap to wash myself. I found that once I had done it I felt much fresher. I put on a clean pair of pants, used my deodorant and dressed myself. I opened the front door to throw out my dirty washing water on the grass verge.

It was beautiful. A fine mist hung over the meadow and the fresh smell of damp vegetation hit my nostrils. Not the cloying clogging smell of petrol fumes, but the sweet smell of grass on a spring morning; still damp and dewy from the night before. I took a deep breath and enjoyed the sensual smell.

Back in the downstairs room I looked about. It was a shame he had not seen the potential in this, it was a large room. Although it suffered from a severe lack of light made worse by the fact he had chose to put the plaster boards against the largest windows in that room so they obscured the light. If I could have moved them alone, I would have done so, but I could not. I think he had put them there so as to stop Pascal knowing he was at home. Silly really, because his van parked outside told everyone that he was inside.

Tony wasn't coming that day; he would return tomorrow which was Friday, so I carried on removing the ivy that was clinging to the house. The stonework needed pointing badly and there were places where there were large holes as the mortar had long since crumbled. I had taken out the necessary tools to do this, but first I was going to practise on the steps leading up to the house. That way, if I made a complete mess of it, we could plant some shrubs in front to cover the pointing up. The pointing was in desperate need of repair on the steps, and eroded rather badly. I think that was because it flooded once a year and nearly covered the steps. Water is a very destructive force. A couple of the stones on the corner of the steps were loose and I would need to rebuild those. But first of all I had to remove all of the weeds that had taken a foothold in the steps, and rake out any loose mortar. Somehow a Russian vine had managed to get a foothold and that was sprouting out everywhere. 'A' decided to carry on with plaster boarding in Clara's bedroom.

It took me a while and it was a tedious painstaking job but I kept at it. Periodically I would have to go and help 'A' with the plaster boarding. I was dismayed when I went into Clara's room. There was plaster board dust everywhere covering my nice clean bed sheets. Why couldn't he have covered the bed before he started? He worked very slowly. I know it wasn't easy cutting plaster board to fit between the beams, but he was so anal about it I could see why he had spent months on plaster boarding five years earlier. Surely professionals were not this precise. I would have thought the odd gap here and there could be filled when the plasterers came along. I had to clean up when he finished.

Chapter 17

The next day Tony arrived and he bought some playmobil stuff with him that his daughter had donated for Clara. It was very nice of him, and I told him so. Clara was overjoyed as she didn't have much to play with, and she got very bored while I was working. I had planned to put her into the local school, but to be honest I was just making sure that 'A' was on his best behaviour and wasn't going to tell us to leave. I would have felt pretty stupid having enrolled her in school only to disappear into the sunset. I told Tony that I was now using the bottled water to make drinks, and he was to help himself. He looked relieved. I think he had seen the algae infested container and had not fancied a hot drink.

We left and went into *Carhaix* to Le Clerc. We were planning a trip to *Ty Recoup* later which I was looking forward to. I went and bought a box of chocolates for Tony's daughter as a thank you for the Playmobil stuff and bought a postcard for Clara to write. We were killing time until *Ty Recoup* opened at 2pm, so we visited McDonalds again much to my horror.

Ty Recoup is a large charity warehouse where people donate furniture and mainly household stuff. 'A' had all his furniture from there. Five years ago, I had persuaded him to buy a large oak table from there for forty Euros. There was a lot of rubbish, but there are some real bargains to be had. We sat outside in the van waiting for the doors to open. We were not alone and a crowd gathered by the roller shutter door. They were closed on Thursday and this was the day when they usually replenished their stock, which explained the eager bargain hunters waiting outside. As soon as the roller shutters went up there was a mad scramble and everyone darted inside. We followed. There was nothing that caught our eye that day. I was looking for suitable furniture for the kitchen area. I had read many years before, that it is pointless having a fitted kitchen in these old stone houses as the damp in the walls turns the MDF to mush very quickly. I also was of the firm belief that the kitchen would eventually move into the annexe if I had anything to do with it. So for now it was better to have freestanding units. There was no furniture suitable, there was nothing to be had that day. I bought a couple of ramekin dishes for 10 cents each.

We got back to the house and I carried on outside. It was very hot and 'A' was inside playing with Clara. He had spent so little time with her over the last few years, that it was good that they were enjoying each other's company. I had told him that I didn't care if he didn't want to do any work, but I did, and it was a change for me to be able to do something without being interrupted by Clara. A couple of years earlier I had secured myself an allotment, and whilst I loved it, Clara hated it with a passion on account of the nettles.

I was weeding the area around the stop tap, and Tony had finished for the day and he left. He had to come back the next week and finish off, but we now had electric lights downstairs. I cannot tell you how joyous we felt, to be able to flick on a switch and see the room illuminated.

After 'A' had cracked open the wine, and was feeling happy from the triumph of electric lights, I put it to him that life would be so much easier with running water. After all, we now had lights, why not running water as well?

I honestly didn't expect him to buy the idea so readily. He had just spent over three thousand euro's on having a wood burner installed (that still didn't work), and having the house wired, so I thought he would be tightening his wallet but to my surprise he seemed to buy into it. Perhaps it was because I said that we could do it ourselves cheaply.

He came outside with me to look at it. "What did you have in mind about getting it into the house?" he said.

"Ah," said I, "I have been thinking about that one."

And I had, quite extensively over the past couple of months as it happened, so I went on to tell him my plans. The previous owner had very thoughtfully put a lot of pipes under the new concrete floor in the downstairs, and then had the floor tiled. Some of them were clearly waste pipes and some were copper pipes for water, and it seemed only sensible to use them. The only problem was that we had never met the man and had no idea which pipes he had intended to use for what; but that aside, we could still use them. First of all we had to get the water into the annexe to join up with the pipes under the main room floor, as they came out into the annexe. This would either be achieved by digging under the three foot thick stone wall, or digging a trench over to where the existing door was and going in through there. It would mean digging a trench of around eight feet, but to my mind it was the surest bet.

'A' was listening intently to my plans. "I think I would prefer to go under the wall," he said. I might have known he would disagree with me so I said nothing. But secretly I was worried. We sipped our wine and looked at the problem and agreed we would make a start in the morning.

The next morning it was drizzling. 'A' had decided to go with my suggestion and take it in through the doorway so he started digging a trench. But then he came to the door and to our horror he uncovered a large stone, in the doorway that had got covered with years of debris that had turned into compost obscuring the stone. There was no way we were going under that, as the edges were under the walls each side of the door.

"What I would like to know is what the original owner was planning to do, as he had the mains put there," said 'A'.

We stood there looking at the position of the stop tap.

"That's what I would like to know too," I said, "but I think he faced the same problem as us, and didn't know what to do about it, as surely he would have had running water in the house if it was easy. He had the pipes put in."

"Let's have a coffee and then I will get to it. We have no choice but to go under the wall."

I was daunted by this prospect, but surprisingly 'A' seemed up to the challenge. I went and made us coffees and I rolled a fag to smoke. I was concerned that this would turn into a nightmare, and end in a blazing row. All I could do was to be as helpful as I possibly could, keep Clara entertained and from whingeing and be as positive as I could muster. Not an easy task.

We went outside and 'A' started to dig a hole between the foundations of the annexe and the square concrete hole that housed the stop tap. The space was about 12 inches, which made using a conventional shovel out of the question. 'A' sat on the wet grass and started using a hand trowel and a pick. The ground was very stony and the going was slow and arduous. He went down about 18 inches before he hit the bottom of the foundations. I gave him a pair of Tony's work gloves that he had left in the house to use. "What about Tony?" said 'A'.

"Fuck Tony. You are going to ruin your hands if you don't wear gloves. You are paying him over two grand for the wiring, I am sure he won't mind you having a pair of work gloves worth less than a quid."

I was seriously worried that this was going to be unsuccessful, and would only succeed in pushing 'A' further down into the spiral of despair, but I kept these misgivings to myself. I just kept the praise coming. After a couple of hours 'A' was on his stomach with his hand inside a tunnel he had dug under the stone wall. He was getting very dirty, but there was no avoiding it. He had to pull handfuls of dirt and stones out one at a time. The stone wall was three feet thick. "I don't know whether to start from the other side," he said. "It is nearly as far as I can reach now, surely I must be nearly at the other side of the wall."

Clara was getting bored and impatient and I was getting anxious. It could all go horribly wrong at any moment. "Have a break for bit," I said.

"No Joanne, I am nearly there, I must be nearly there. I am going in from the other side."

We went into the house and opened the door to the annexe. It was a shabby modern chipboard internal door. There was no light. "Take the oak log down that is propping the door and move that door that will let some light in. We can't keep going through the house." I said thinking of my newly mopped floor. 'A' saw the sense in this and did as I had suggested. There still wasn't enough light, so he got the freestanding halogen floor lamp that his neighbour Julien had given him years ago and put it in the annexe.

The annexe was full of crap. The floor was covered in large stones, no doubt from the ruins attached to the annexe. The previous owner had been getting ready to put a concrete floor down, but it was uneven and difficult to traverse. There were two steps down into the annex from the main house. Everywhere there was debris, a large tree stump that had some kind of heavy metal machinery attached to it. "What the hell do you think that is?" said 'A'.

"I have absolutely no idea," I replied.

"Whatever it is, it weighs a ton," said 'A' as he tried to move it out of the way. "Do you think it is some priceless antique? We could do with the money."

"I doubt it knowing our luck. It looks like a pile of rusty old crap to me," and we both started laughing.

When we had cleared the way we stood looking at the corner of the room. "I have no idea where we are going to come through the wall," said 'A'.

"I will go and get your tape measure. If we measure the distance from the hole to the doorway on the outside and then measure inside the same amount it should give us a rough idea."

When we had measured, we realised that we were coming through in the corner of the annexe, so 'A' started digging there. A great hairy arsed spider ran away inches from 'A''s face as he was again lying on his belly. I winced but said nothing.

"There is a big stone in the way," said 'A' "I am going outside to see if I can push through. I want you to get the torch to look down the hole and see if you can see anything."

I winced again, the thought of having to lie down on that floor, after I had just seen that spider was horrifying, but I knew I had to do it. "Hang on a second," I said, "I am just going to get the picnic blanket from the car." At least I could keep relatively clean. I couldn't fail him now. I hadn't seen him this motivated for a long time.

With me installed belly down on the picnic blanket inside the annexe, and 'A' outside working away we communicated by shouting. "I can hear you using the poker on the stone."

"Can you see anything Joanne?" he shouted back.

I got the torch, but the hole was too deep and at an angle. "No," I shouted.

"I am going to put some water down the hole and see what happens." he shouted back.

"The water is coming through," I called out and I got up and went outside. "You must be nearly there if there is water coming through." It was nearly 1pm. "Let's have some lunch and then we can have another go. Have a break." The last thing I wanted was a 'hangry' man on my hands. "You need a break from lying on your stomach."

He agreed, and I made some lunch. I was getting worried that this would all amount to nothing. My greatest fear was that some ruddy great stone was in the way and all the mornings work would be in vain, and 'A' would be pissed off for the rest of the day. But he was as determined as ever, and as soon as he had finished his lunch was back at it again. I washed up and then went outside to see what was happening. "How are you doing?" I said.

"I don't know Joanne," and he disappeared into the annexe. "Come here will you?" he called.

I wondered what the hell had gone wrong when I walked into the annexe. "Can you have a look down that hole for me, can you see anything?" He said. I got the torch and peered down the hole. There was the pipe! He had done it.

We cracked open the wine early that day in celebration just as the rain began to pour outside.

Chapter 18

The next morning was brighter, and the rain that had been pouring for most of the night had stopped. It was lovely to see all the vegetation glistening with rain, and the sun could be seen casting its golden glow on the horizon.

'A' had decided that he needed a wash, and long overdue if you ask me. I don't think he noticed that he had a slight odour to him, or perhaps he had, hence the wash. 'A' didn't do as I did, and have a strip wash with a flannel and soap. He got a bucket of hot water, and downstairs on the tiled floor used a jug to tip it over him. He didn't want either Clara or I to see him in a state of undress, so we went for a walk while he was having a wash and sloshing water everywhere.

I had been up to the top meadow one evening earlier in the week to have a look if anything remained of the orchard. 'A' said he hadn't looked, as the previous year he saw little left of it. Instead of the healthy four year old trees he had planned to see, he said there was nothing left. Even though I had doubted the orchard had been sited correctly, I was surprised that not one of the trees had survived. So I had decided to look for myself.

I did manage to find about five trees, which was what was left of the thirteen trees we had planted five years earlier. They were smaller than when we had planted them. They stood about two feet high, and it was clear that they had been constantly nibbled. I felt sad. Pascal had told 'A' (after he had planted the trees), that they needed protection from deer. Another laugh at our expense, and it was something 'A' had not heeded. That in itself was odd. Why listen to his advice about where to plant them, and then not listen to the advice about deer? I think it was the cost of protecting them against the deer that was a step too far in 'A''s book. But looking at those trees, or what was left of them, I didn't think it was deer. Madame Le Jeune grazed her horses in that meadow using an electric fence. When we had planted them, 'A' had asked her to move the fence so that the horses couldn't touch the trees, which she had the time, but what about after he had gone?

We walked down the lane that Sunday morning and to my utter surprise there were horses back grazing in the top meadow. Not just one or two, but five. When had they arrived? They weren't there in the week, and we would have noticed a big fuck-off horse box coming down the lane. The electric fence was up and running, and closed off his meadow. She had also taken the liberty of putting rudimentary fencing around the bottom meadow. She was obviously using that one as well, and now there was a large water container in there. My blood began to boil. I couldn't wait to get back to the house.

"There are horses in the top meadow again." I said to 'A' who seemed unconcerned. I continued "You would think she would have the common courtesy to stop by the house and ask if it was alright?"

"They must have arrived when we were out." Was 'A''s reply.

"Well there was a car there when I came back from my walk, and it passed me as I was outside the front of the house. There was a woman driving it, she could have stopped and had a word then. It is really taking the piss. If you only charged 25 Euros a week per horse that is 500 Euros a month and that is an income. I wouldn't mind but they are fine horses, not shitty little ponies."

"This is really winding you up isn't it?" said 'A'. It was true, it had wound me up. That and the water all over the floor from 'A''s wash, which I was now mopping up, had pissed me right off.

"It seems that the electric fence is not preventing the horses from grazing near what is left of your trees either," said I.

I was clearly getting to 'A'. "Will you forget it, Joanne," he said, "you are so wound up, and it is winding me up too. I am not in a position to piss the locals off, as I have no septic tank and I don't want them to tip me off to the authorities."

He had a point I suppose, so I left it, but it really made me angry that they were grazing their horses for free.

I calmed down, eventually, and cooked a roast chicken. I still hadn't got my head around the high price of vegetables, so we had tinned peas and carrots from Lidl as veg. I normally like a cauliflower cheese on my Sunday lunch, but the cauliflowers were nearly 3 Euros, something I found exorbitant when they were less than a pound back home. This is quite surprising as quite a lot of our cauliflowers come from Brittany. We didn't do much that day. We sat in bed and watched films in the afternoon and I prepared a shopping list for the next day.

The next morning, I was tackling the thorny problem of the chemical toilet and the emptying thereof. 'A' had been using sawdust in the bottom of the porta-potti, and using it for solids only. He had been using a bucket to pee in. Whilst I don't mind using a bucket to pee in, our eight year old daughter did not. I suspect 'A' had been using sawdust, because he didn't like emptying the toilet.

Years previously, when he had the caravan, I had emptied the toilet up at the village campsite. Calling it a campsite is a little bit of an exaggeration, as it is just basically a car park next to the community centre and sports field that was designed for motor homes and touring caravans to stay overnight, or at most a couple of days. 'A' had told me that the toilet up there was now locked permanently, and you had to obtain the key from the *Mairie's* office, something which he did not want to do as it was highlighting the fact that he had no septic tank. I did point out that they must wonder what he was doing with his shit, and would be re-assured he was using a chemical toilet, but he wasn't convinced with my thinking on the matter. So he had taken to emptying it when he had to in *Carhaix Plouguer* at the public toilets on the car park in the main square.

I was going to empty it, and then use the 'chem blue' that I had bought out with me, and from then on would empty it once a week on a Monday on our shopping/washing run.

We loaded the van up, and I have to say that the toilet hummed, and I was sat in the back with it. After stopping off at the recycle bin on the way, our next stop was the public toilets. Thankfully, there were not many people on the car park and 'A' parked directly outside of the toilets. I shot inside to make sure that no one else was in there, and after a quick look to see if anyone was about, we got the toilet inside. I needed 'A''s help to do this as it was rather heavy.

If you have ever been to France and experienced their public toilets you will know what to expect, but for those of you that haven't, I will explain. In addition to a few toilet cubicles (if you are lucky), they have what is known as a toilet *à la turque*. It basically looks like a shower tray with a largish hole in the centre near the back. I think you are supposed to squat. This was where I was going to empty the toilet, which I did as fast as I could. The sawdust had turned the effluent into a sludge. I was horrified, and just hoped it didn't block the toilet. When I pressed the flush, the sludge came up into the shower tray. I was mortified, but when it settled I flushed again. Thankfully this time it went down, but I was still worried that it would indeed cause someone else a problem. At least the damn toilet was now empty, and from now on with the aid of chemicals it would empty easier.

Although, after that I dreaded the weekly emptying ritual. There was something about it that made me feel uneasy. We were foreigners, and it felt like we were doing something illegal, although I don't think we were. I imagined being caught and hauled before the local magistrate for emptying a toilet, and all the tittering, jeering and shaking of heads that would ensue. We nicknamed ourselves the toilet bandits after a few weeks of this.

Relieved that the toilet had been emptied without us being caught, we went on to do the shopping and washing. Before, 'A' had only probably only done one load of washing a week; you know ladies, all the coloureds and whites and towels mixed in together. But now, we did at least three loads of washing. The cost was mounting, and it was coming out of my housekeeping. I suggested that we buy a rotary close line for outside, which would pay for itself in a matter of weeks because we didn't have to pay for the cost of drying.

I had my list and I shopped whilst 'A' and Clara sat in the cafe. Bacon was a problem. They only sold streaky rashers, but that morning I found something in the packaged cooked meats section that looked like thinly sliced bacon medallions. As they are smoked, the French use them uncooked in sandwiches I realised, after looking at the sandwich stall in the supermarket. I found out that these were an excellent replacement for our usual British bacon. They had no fat and just needed a few minutes heat in the frying pan. I was getting the hang of shopping in France and I had quickly adapted to their produce, but it was still relatively expensive compared to that at home. But the wine was cheap and very good.

We went to the *Bricolage* in search of plumbing fittings, but after ten minutes it was apparent that despite receiving a little lesson from my son on the joys of push-fit plumbing, we didn't have the foggiest what to do. We needed a flexible pipe to go under the wall and my rudimentary lessons had not included that. To my surprise 'A' decided that we needed the help of a professional. I was relieved.

Thankfully when we got back to the house Tony was hard at work. I had apologised that morning for taking his work gloves, and had offered him the money for them. Of course, he declined as I expected he would. Although he was quiet at first, he became friendly as time went on. I would like to think it was my influence, as I am rather 'up front' about things, but I can only guess at that. On our return home, I explained what we had been doing at the weekend (with regards trying to get running water into the house) and asked him if he knew of anyone who would be able and willing to do the job. I had asked 'A' about Vic, who had installed the wood burner, but it was apparent with what 'A' had said about him, that he would not be interested in a piddling job like that, so we needed someone else.

Tony did indeed know of someone who was just starting out, and he promised to email me his number when he got home. Notice that he said he would email me. It was difficult to say the least at the house with no mobile signal, and therefore no internet. I am still not sure whether it was because we were in a valley, or because the stone walls were three foot thick. I occasionally got a signal upstairs, and it was better if I went outside but it would cut out at the drop of a hat. It was infuriating to say the least.

The weather was picking up again and I had been in France for nearly two weeks and so far 'A' had behaved; it looked like we were staying, so it made sense to enrol Clara in school. I was finding it hard to occupy her, and do work at the same time. I know it makes me sound like a shit parent, and to be honest I felt like one; I did spend time with her, as did 'A', but we couldn't give over all of our time to entertain her, as we had work to do.

I have to confess that I am really quite a shy person. I have learnt to overcome this over the years, but I still find it hard to confront new situations, and I have to work myself up to it, as it were. That day was no different, and I spent the whole day working myself up to it. It had the added anxiety that my daughter, who was eight, was about to be thrown into the deep end in a French speaking school, and I was feeling anxious for her. The only thing that helped me with all of this was that she had confessed that she was bored, and wanted to go to school. Ignorance is bliss, so they say and I consoled myself with the fact that she wanted to go. It didn't stop me worrying, as I changed into something more respectable and put on some lipstick to go up to the school.

We went in the van. That itself put us on a back burner. All was quiet up in the sleepy hollow that is *Cleden Poher*. We parked and rang the school doorbell, and were greeted by a plump and pleasant young woman who was the head mistress. I spoke in pigeon French for the best part and I was glad that I did, because her English was non-existent. Between us, I managed to ascertain that yes she would take Clara and she could start on Thursday. She gave me some forms to complete, but said that it didn't matter if I didn't fill them all in by Thursday. I managed to glean from the notices on the wall behind her that they didn't have school on Wednesdays. Could this be true? I felt sure I had missed something, but the menus of the school lunches stopped on Tuesday and resumed on Thursday.

It was a lovely school. It had a warm feeling about it and it was calm and serene. I could hear no screaming kids, and the building itself was filled with light and was clean and inviting. How different to England. The performance I had on my return to get Clara back into her old school made me actually think they didn't want her to go to school, yet here in France it was as if "okay, wonderful she can start straight away."

Tony had given us the name of a plumber who was English and was just starting out, so I had left him a voicemail telling him what we wanted, and asking him to call. When we climbed back into the van I checked my phone. It had become a habit, because the signal was so poor down in the valley, but up on the hill it was fine. I had a missed call, and it was from Wayne the plumber, so I phoned him back and left another voicemail. It would appear that he had problems with a mobile signal too.

Chapter 19

The weather had turned gloriously warm and sunny, and we decided to visit the seaside the next day as a treat for Clara, who would start school on Thursday. Between us we had managed to fill in the forms for the school, and felt rather chuffed with ourselves having got over this little hurdle of French bureaucracy.

Cleden Poher is a little left of centre in the wedge that is Brittany, and as such it is about fifty miles from the coast to the north, south and west. We had plenty of places to choose from, but I wanted to go to *Bénodet,* as it is a popular south coastal resort in Brittany for tourists. I had seen some lovely photos on the internet before I came out. So with a picnic rug, towel, bucket and spade and a packed lunch we set off a little after 9am; me as usual, in the back of the van 'hill billy' style.

We drove through wide open spaces on the large roads that are the equivalent of our motorways here, and in no time at all we were driving along the coast road on our way to *Bénodet* . *Bénodet* is so called because it sits at the mouth of the river *Odet*. As we approached *Bénodet*, we saw an increasing number of palm trees and on a sunny day it is a very pretty seaside town. Clara and I were quite excited when we parked the van, having driven past the seafront. It is a large sandy bay and there is a little promenade with shops, restaurants and bars. It was fairly quiet as it was midweek. Something that struck me in particular, was the large amount of beach huts lining the beach and the concrete boardwalk. There were, also to my surprise showers. It was a nice beach, but I could see that in the midst of holiday season it would be heaving with holidaymakers and that would somewhat mar the beauty of it. There was an ice cream kiosk on the promenade, and we stopped and bought an ice cream before we went onto the beach.

I am not really a fan of ice cream, but all manner of exotic flavours were to be had at that stall. Pistachio, white chocolate and raspberry, blueberry, coffee mocha just to name a few, but when I saw rum and raisin I was sold. I still remember rum and raisin choc ices from my childhood. I know that puts me in the severely old category, but God did I love 'em.

We licked our ice creams and sat on the sand. It was a beautiful day for a beach, and I reclined on the picnic rug letting the sun warm my face as I thought, while Clara and her father went in search of shells.

I was loving France. What was there not to love? I was living in a rural idyll (albeit with no sanitation, but that was a minor point for me) that had the coast on three sides of us and was only an hour's drive away. The warmth of the sun was really relaxing and I dug my body into the sand making a little bed. How could anyone not love this?

'A' didn't love it. That was pretty obvious. I don't know what he does like to be honest, apart from lying in bed, reading a book or watching a film and being fed like a baby or an old man on a tray. It is harsh I know, what I am about to say, but I concluded that he would be better off in a care home. Only he wouldn't like that. The trouble is that there is no pleasing some people. There is an old saying that you only get out of life what you put in, and I believe wholeheartedly that it is true. He was always grumbling and complaining about how life had dealt him a bum deal. Well from where I was standing, life had dealt me a pretty bum deal too, and probably worse than his, but I wasn't complaining. I loved every minute of it. There are people in this world who through some cruel twist of fate are unable to travel, unable to walk and reliant on others for their every need. How dare he complain about his lot.

I lifted my head from the sand and opened my eyes to watch him and Clara on the beach. I felt truly sorry for him, but I had tried my best and there was nothing else I could do. I would make the most of my time in France, because like everything else that is lovely in life, it comes to an end sooner or later.

They showed no sign of coming back to where I was sitting, and 'A' had indeed sat down on the sand some way up the beach. I took this as a sign of indignation on the part of 'A', having got fed up with the search for shells. Clara was still at the water's edge looking. I got up, dusted myself down, picked up the rug and bag and walked over to them.

He confessed he had had enough of the beach. I could have stayed there for a couple more hours at least and so could Clara, because she was sad when I said we had to go.

We had a beer at a cafe at 'A''s request, and I wished we hadn't, because he moaned about the price later.

But he was hot, and he was glad when we got back to the house.

That evening I think he had sensed my disappointment, because he said he had been hot on the beach, by way of an explanation.

I didn't take any notice, because tomorrow was school for Clara. French school no less, and we needed an early night.

French school starts at 8.50am. There was no school uniform which was a plus for Clara. You have to pay for the school meals, but they were on par with prices back home, only they billed you for them afterwards, you didn't pay in advance, and what fine meals they were. One and a half hours for lunch, and a three course meal. It surprised me, but the starter was often a salad or vegetable based; tomatoes with garlic, olive oil and basil, or tabbouleh, or celeriac salad, or something similar. It was always served with French bread. The main meal was meat and a carbohydrate; either potatoes, rice or pasta and then followed by desert. It was so lovely; I would have gladly eaten it myself.

The plus side was school didn't finish until 4.30pm, on account of the extended lunch break. Yippee! I would get a load of work done. I was able to take her in to her classroom and kiss her goodbye. She seemed pleased to be with kids of her own age, and away from her grumpy old father. I went back to the house to continue stripping ivy from the outside walls, and raking out the joints in between the stones on the wall, whilst 'A' continued plaster boarding Clara's room.

It wasn't long before he came out and asked me for my help. I couldn't really say no. I think he missed the company, but it was tedious. I had to help him hold up bits of plasterboard so that he could mark them before he cut them. Then he would hold them back up again and trim off a bit more and then use a rasp to make a good fit. I came to realise that he was a perfectionist. Surely it wouldn't matter if there were little gaps?

He had two speeds, slow and stop. No wonder it had taken him so long to achieve what he had. He kept mislaying his tools. He would put them down somewhere, and not be able to find them. It was my job to get them for him, so I kept tabs on where he put them to try and speed things up. I also tidied as we worked, putting the slithers of plasterboard in bags and sweeping up when necessary. I was slightly irritated, because I wanted to start pointing and he didn't really need my help, but I went along with it and tried to be patient.

I worried about Clara all day, but I needn't have, as she was full of excitement when I collected her from school. She couldn't wait to tell me all about it; my heartfelt happy that she was having a good time and I relaxed a little.

After I had dropped Clara off at school the next day, we went into *Carhaix*. 'A' needed some supplies from the *bricolage* and we needed more wine and food for the weekend. It was good to be out without Clara, and I had a coffee in the *cafè* at Le Clerc with 'A' while he perused his emails.

Many years earlier, I had suggested that he have two velux windows fitted in the roof of the house on the back side. Where he had decided to place the bathroom, meant that it had no window in at all, as it was under the eaves for the most part. He had said all those years ago, that he didn't want any velux windows, but now that he had partitioned the rooms upstairs, he could see the sense in this and had decided after all, that he did want a velux. He had made steps the week earlier (unknown to me) to contact a roofer, and he announced as we sipped our coffees that Sean was coming tomorrow to quote for the velux, the leak in the roof and replacing the guttering.

There had been a slight leak in the roof for years near the chimney breast, as you may recall from earlier chapters, and this was something that needed fixing. While it didn't seem a problem in the summer, come the autumn and the winter, the rain would piss it down. The guttering at the front of the house was made of zinc, as is the custom in France and it was full of holes. This wasn't an urgent job but he could quote for it at the same time.

The next day (Saturday), I did some jobs and we had lunch. Sean said he was coming in the afternoon. This could mean anything from midday to 5pm, and Clara was chomping at the bit to go to McDonalds for her weekly Happy Meal fix. I decided to clear off the stone steps at the side of the house. They were overgrown with weeds and moss, and although we didn't use them regularly as the ladder/staircase was now operational, we did use them to take plaster board upstairs and to get the porta-potti out on a Monday for emptying. They were not very safe.

I worked on them for a couple of hours around by 'piss corner' as we named it. So called, because this was where 'A' went for a pee in the day. It was okay when it rained, but when it had been dry and hot for a few days, as it had recently, it stank of piss. I just hoped the locals didn't get a whiff of it when they walked past, and that it would rain again soon.

The stairs were desperately in need of pointing and repair, I noted as I cleared away the weeds and moss. This was yet another job to add to my never ending list of work that I wanted to do. I stood no chance of getting these jobs completed if I continually had to help' 'A plaster board. Still what could I do about it? I would just have to keep plodding on with what I could, when I could.

The idea of having the velux installed at this time was a sound one, because of the soil being built up behind the house. This avoided the requirement of a ladder to get to the back of the roof. It also made sense to install the window while the weather was good, as in the other months of the year the chances of it pissing it down were greatly increased.

I finished at about 3pm and was wondering when the hell this bloke would turn up. I stood over by my car, on the other side of the road and stood looking at the house itself. It was looking better with the vegetation removed, and I couldn't wait to see what it looked like when I pointed it. A beat up old BMW with Irish plates came down the lane and parked at an angle in the middle of the lane, a little way up. A thin, rangy looking man got out wearing a t-shirt that was full of holes. I realised that it must be the roofer.

"Hi yah, lovely day isn't it?" said the bloke, so I shouted 'A', who was in the house, and he quickly appeared.

'A' came out to meet him and I gestured to Sean that 'A' was the person he should see. 'A' took him in the house. I'm afraid to say that I took an instant disliking to Sean, and didn't trust him one little bit. I stayed put on the grass verge and could hear 'A' talking to Sean inside the house. Just then they appeared at the bedroom window. "Do you mind if I go and have a look?" said Sean in his Paul O Grady voice, and he leapt out of the bedroom window and onto the roof in an act of what I thought was rash stupidity. I thought he was trying to impress, but it certainly didn't have that effect on me, it just made me more doubtful of his abilities as a professional.

After prancing about on the roof for a bit, he went inside and he and 'A' emerged a few seconds later through the front door. He was inspecting the guttering. "How long do you think that is?" he asked A. I couldn't believe my ears. "Have you got a tape measure?" he asked 'A'. For God's sake, the man had come to quote for a job, and he hadn't even got a tape measure with him.

After they had measured, they came across the road to where I stood. Sean started to talk to me. He obviously realised that I was not impressed with him.

"I think it just needs a bit of silicone at the edge of that window frame that is all. That will cure the leak." He said.

"So you don't think it is the pointing on the chimney then?" I replied.

He looked up at the chimney, "oh that needs pointing," he said, stating the bleeding obvious. "There are weeds growing out of it. I will soon have that sorted. I was just telling your husband."

I cut him off before he could continue. "We are not married, we are just friends."

"Oh well, I was just saying that I am really busy at the moment, but if he wants to get a velux window, then Brico Depot is the best place." Sean continued.

"I don't think I have seen a Brico Depot around here," I replied.

"There is one in *Quimper* and in *Morlaix*, I think," said Sean. He said he would email 'A' the quote and shot off rather quickly as there was another car in the lane and his beat up old BMW was blocking the road.

Clara was relieved, because now she could go and have her McDonalds. Once in the van 'A' started talking. "I liked him," he said.

"Did you?" was all I said.

"I take it you didn't then?" said 'A'.

"It doesn't really matter what I think, it is your house. I could be wrong, I just don't agree with his diagnosis about the leak. I am of the firm belief that it is coming from the chimney or the ridge tiles by the chimney. Water doesn't run uphill does it? But hey, beggars can't be choosers and around here it is difficult enough to get anyone to do any work for you. We will see what his quote says."

"Yeh," said 'A', "we could go to Brico Depot on Wednesday and we could visit a beach up on that stretch of the coast while we are there if you like. We could make an outing of it, being as it is quite a distance."

Chapter 20

The house was old. According to 'A', the earliest records of it were in the 1700's. One of Vic Beans sidekicks who had come with him had told 'A' that the house would have originally had a thatched roof. He knew this because of the slates sticking out of the stonework above the upstairs door. From little bits of evidence and firsthand accounts by locals who knew *Le Ster*, I suspected that it had been a grain store. It's proximity to the canal for a start, when barges would have formed a transportation system. The outside steps leading to the upstairs and the large upstairs door that had originally been there. There was also a very old large stone trough outside, which would have been for the horses that drew the carts. Grain would have been stored on the first floor and the occupants would have lived on the ground floor.

Many people had lived there over the years. Julien's wife who was local, had told 'A' that peasants had occupied the house for many years and had kept their animals in the annexe. They had grown vegetables where the filtration plant was to be sited. It must have been a poor existence, as that spot was shaded. But it was very romantic to imagine how it would have been a couple hundred years ago. There had originally been a road that ran past *Le Ster* from the top of the hill. It would have been a gentler gradient for the horses than the modern one, which was straight and rose rapidly. That road had almost disappeared and had been consumed by fields and woodlands; just here and there remnants of it remained. Many people had lived and died in that house and it had seen a lot over its lifetime. That in itself was a romantic notion that made me love the house.

The weather broke on Sunday and it rained all day. I did nothing apart from re-organise the kitchen and cook roast pork. Calling it a kitchen was a bit of an exaggeration.

The downstairs of the house is a large room of approximately 9 metres by 8 metres. You entered through the front door and in front of you and just slightly left of the middle of the room, was the stairs. Given the low roof and the beams, 'A' had done his best to make the stairs out of oak. I know that I had had my misgivings about them, but actually they worked quite well. They had no hand rail and were a cross between a ladder and stairs, but it was better than going outside. To the right of the stairs and on the side wall, was the massive fireplace that housed the log burner. To the left of the stairs, a space that was approximately a third of the entire room, was where 'A' planned to have his kitchen.

Presently it was arranged like this: On your immediate left as soon as you entered the house was the fridge, with its back against the front wall of the house. On top of the fridge sat the kettle. Then there was a small space and a small window. On the left hand side of the room stood the sink. It was an old Belfast sink that 'A' had found at *Ty Recoup* in *Rostrenan* and it still stood on the breezeblocks that I had suggested five years ago. Next to it was the cooker and then next to that was two low cupboards. Both of which I hated with a passion. The first cupboard was so difficult to open that I had to hold it steady with one hand whilst wrenching the knob on the door with my other hand. For a start off, they were hideously ugly and

I suspected 'A' had chosen them for their price tag, rather than their aesthetic qualities. They were also too small to be of any use in a kitchen, and were really bedside cabinets.

I decided that I was going to put these two small cabinets next to the fridge, and put one on top of the other and take the doors off the one that was difficult to open, it hacked me off no end. The cupboards largely acted as a protection against mice. Previously 'A' had had a mouse problem. I had seen evidence once or twice of mouse droppings on the drainer, shortly my arrival, but I had thoroughly bleached it and made sure that I didn't leave any washing up about, and that the bins were emptied every evening after dinner. I would only use the open fronted cupboard for saucepans in any event not food.

Although I hadn't originally been sold on a freestanding kitchen, I decided that it wasn't such a bad idea after all. I knew that there was no use having a fitted kitchen against these old walls as the units would absorb the damp and soon disintegrate like cardboard. I also had still not got over the idea that one day the annex would be restored and I could have a massive kitchen in there. It would happen one day even if I had to use some of my future inheritance to do it. What I really wanted was an old sideboard or buffet as they are called in France. Every time we went into *Carhaix* we looked in *Ty Recoup* to see if we could find one. There was a lot of rubbish in there, but there was also some good stuff. The only problem was that there was a dedicated collection of *Ty Recoup* fans, who would be there when the doors opened to snaffle the bargains. I had missed out on a magnificent but slightly battered oak armoire for 50 Euros because I had hesitated. After chewing it over in my mind as a makeshift pantry, by the time I had gone back to get it, it had gone.

There were a lot of sideboards in *Ty Recoup* but they were mainly of the Breton style. Breton style furniture is heavily and ornately carved and thoroughly hideous. It is utterly lacking in taste and there is nothing that you can do to make that furniture decent. Both 'A' and I had decided that we did not want a Breton dresser or sideboard. I was looking for a plain one, preferably with drawers as well as cupboards and of a height that I could use as a work surface. So far we had seen nothing suitable, but I remained hopeful that one day we would happen upon the right piece.

Monday was as usual and I looked forward to getting stuck into work on Tuesday. But Tuesday arrived and 'A' had other ideas.

"I don't feel like doing any plaster boarding today," he said, "why don't we go and get a cake and a coffee at the patisserie in *Carhaix*. But first I would like you to cut my hair."

I was filled with horror. I was certainly no barber, and all I had was scissors and a comb. "Are you sure about this? Wouldn't you prefer a professional to do it?" I asked, hoping he would change his mind.

"Yes, I am sure. I can't go to a barber, because how am I going to tell them what I want?" Well I suppose he had a point, but I would have got my dictionary out and cobbled some suitable phrase together rather than have an amateur cut my hair.

It wasn't a bad job but it wasn't brilliant either. The only thing I could say about it was that it looked neater and I hadn't cut too much off. It is too late when it is on the floor and you can do little about it then.

I was a little disappointed that I hadn't done any work for days. The rain meant that I couldn't do any pointing. Mondays were taken up with emptying the toilet, disposing of the numerous wine bottles we had amassed, washing and shopping. Clara was off on Wednesdays and nothing happened Sundays, which meant that we really had only three days in which to get any work done, and now 'A' was suggesting that we play hooky. But I couldn't very well raise an objection. I couldn't force him to work.

"Okay." I said.

As it happened, the *patisserie* was selling delightful pastries for one euro. How on earth could they make a profit? There were all manner of delectable confections under the counter. Large chocolate éclairs, chocolate millefeulle slices, rum babas, slices of apple flan glazed with apricot conserve, slices of strawberry gateau. I decided on a chocolate millefeulle and 'A' had a rum baba. He said he didn't like the éclairs in France. They filled them with *crème patisserie* not cream, like we do in England. We sat in the cafe eating our cakes and indulging in the free Wi-Fi. I checked my emails. "Wayne has said he can come pop around this afternoon to look at the pipe," I said.

"Great, tell him okay." Replied 'A'. The possibility that we were going to get running water in the house was exciting to say the least.

Wayne and an older man stopped by the house at about 5pm. Wayne was only about thirty, but he drove a van with sign writing on the side proudly proclaiming his trade. He was Cornish, as a lot of ex pats are in Brittany. He had a look at what we wanted.

"We can come on Friday," he said. "It should only take a couple of hours, 300 Euros?"

I was a little shocked, but then everything involving tradesmen was pricey over in Brittany. I was sure that the locals would be cheaper but 'A' wanted to use English tradesmen and given how few there were they had you over a barrel when it came to the price.

"Yes, that's okay," said 'A'.

"Great," said Wayne, "we'll see you on Friday then."

"Well that was easy enough," said 'A'.

"They haven't done it yet," I said. "I will tell you more about it when we have running water."

The next day I made sandwiches and we went in search of Brico Depot in *Morlaix*. We travelled the road that I should have taken on my arrival, if I hadn't missed the turning. We found Brico Depot without much difficulty and it was fantastic; a very large, and very cheap DIY store. We roamed the aisles and surveyed the goods on offer. 'A' picked up some timber for finishing off the boxing underneath the windows upstairs, he also picked up a couple of clamps and then we went in search of a velux window. There were none on display but they had them in the catalogue.

"Well how do you go about buying one?" he said to me.

"I don't know, but let's find out," was my reply. We approached the customer service desk. It was clear that A was a little daunted at the prospect of talking French, so I took over.

"*Bonjour Madame*," I said to the woman behind the desk as way of an opener and then launched myself into full on French. "*Je voudrais un fenetre pour la toit.*" It was not easy as I was far from fluent, but I made myself understood and the woman started gabbling on in French and gesturing.

"Did you catch any of that?" I said as we walked away from the counter.

"I think she said pay for it at the desk and collect it from somewhere outside."

"That was what I thought too," I added and we stood in the queue to pay.

"Thank you for your help Joanne," he said. I felt quite chuffed with myself.

"That place was wonderful," said 'A' as we drove to the beach. "I wish I had known about it earlier."

We arrived at the coast, at a little place called *Carantec*. It was not far from *Roscoff* on the north coast of Brittany. It was drizzling as we got out of the van.

"I like this better than *Bénodet*," said 'A' as we picked our way along the little path that wound down the cliff to the beach. It was a pretty little cove, but the weather somewhat marred my enjoyment. Everything looked so grey.

"Yes, it is nice here but it would probably be better on a sunny day," I replied.

I sat on a rock whilst Clara her father combed the small beach for shells. Quite what I was going to do with all these shells I didn't know, but I would think of something. I remembered being seriously into collecting shells when I was Clara's age. The drizzle started to get heavier and I called them to go. We were going to get soaked if we stayed on the beach. It was absolutely shitty weather for late May hopefully it would break soon and I could get back to working outside.

Friday arrived and so did Wayne and his father-in-law as they had promised. It was pissing it down with rain outside. I felt sorry for them grubbing about outside with the pipe in the pouring rain so I made them a cup of tea.

"Proper tea this is," I said as I handed them the mugs. "I bought a stash over from England when I came."

Despite Wayne saying it would only be a couple of hours they seemed to be having difficulty. Wayne came into the room, "Look, we are going to have to go and get some different pipe. It is nearly lunchtime, so we will go and get the pipe, grab some lunch and come back." Nothing ever went smoothly at *Le Ster*, I had got used to it but 'A' would quickly descend into a downwards spiral whenever we hit an obstacle.

"Okay," said 'A'. "Look, we shall go into *Carhaix* and be back a bit later. I will leave the house open for you."

Wayne and his father-in-law Dave left in the van. "The house will be alright Joanne; your car is outside anyway, no one will know whether we are at home or not. I am sick of sitting in the house and it is Friday at *Ty Recoup*." A loved nothing more than a bit of bargain hunting and we had visited *Ty Recoup* enough to know that Friday was the best day to get a bargain.

Today was no exception and we sat in the van waiting for the roller shutter to go up. Once inside it was fevered excitement with people rushing everywhere looking to grab the latest find before someone else did. I was on the lookout for some dining chairs. We only got one proper one, and we used the folding wooden garden chairs that Pascal had given 'A' when he had first moved in. I had bought a wooden chair with a woven rush seat a week earlier, and it had proven to be very comfortable, so comfortable that Clara and her father fought over who was going to sit on it. So I was on the lookout for more.

I wasn't disappointed and soon found a set of three. They were three Euros each. A was happy enough with them as they put them in the back of the van. There was no sign of a buffet though which was disappointing, we would just have to keep looking.

When we got back to the house Wayne and Dave were back at work.

"Did you have a good lunch?" I asked.

"Yes," said Wayne, "we went to that restaurant on the road out of *Cleden*. It was a fixed price lunch of 13 Euros and it was rather good." It was amazing that the tiny village of *Cleden* had only one *tabac* and a hairdresser as its only shops, yet the village sported three restaurants.

I asked Wayne about the back boiler. 'A' had originally asked him to quote for this as well, but when he came previously he had said that he was still looking into it.

. "Well the problem is that using the back boiler means that it is not a pressurised system and that does not comply with French regulations. Which means my insurance won't cover it. I have asked Jean Pierre at the plumbers merchants to look into it for me, but I don't hold out much hope." 'A' was listening to what Wayne had to say and he was not going to be happy I knew it. Early that morning I had listened to him ranting about having the wood burner and not being able to use it. I had to agree with him that it was bloody annoying. This latest spell of rain meant that it was quite cold in the mornings and at night and it was just the time you could do with having the log burner on for a while. In order to keep warm whilst having my daily wash I had taken to putting the oven on and leaving the door open. I jokingly called it 'the gas fire'.

"This is bloody typical," said 'A'. "I finally get that wood burner fitted and I can't use it. Vic Bean fucks off and doesn't want to come back and fit the plumbing. Are you suggesting I just scrap the boiler? Oh dear, I thought. He was very angry.

"No," said Wayne, I am still looking into it. I just said that my insurance wouldn't cover it. I haven't given up yet." I could understand Wayne's point of view, but 'A' was fuming.

"When I first bought this place five years ago, I had a plumber come around and he advised me to have a log burner with a back boiler, so I spent over a grand on that log burner and when I phoned the plumber up I was told that he had moved back to England. I have been misadvised. Then I had a bloody heart attack and then Brexit. It has ruined all of my ideas of retirement." Said 'A'.

"Calm down," I said. I was really worried that he was going to give himself another heart attack. "Look Wayne, he is not having a pop at you, he is just very stressed about the wood burner. I mean it doesn't matter to us if it doesn't comply with French regulations. Is that a problem for you?" Thankfully, 'A' said nothing.

"Well no not really. The only thing is it would be a problem if you came to sell the house," said Wayne.

"Well, we are not planning to do that any time soon, and it would be nice to get the hot water on." 'A' seemed satisfied for now and he appeared to have calmed down. Wayne went back to fitting the tap.

Things were moving forward now, and Wayne was soldering copper pipe near the sink for the tap, I was actually beginning to think that this was really going to happen. Then disaster struck. There were numerous pipes sticking out of the floor in the kitchen. 'A' had thought that the original owner had laid them in the concrete floor ready to connect to the plumbing for the rest of the house. There were about three coming up in the back left hand corner which 'A' had surmised were for the bathroom. At the present time they were hidden by a wooden bench and tools stacked in the corner of the room. When Wayne turned the water on it came spurting out of the pipe behind the bench like a geyser.

"Turn the water off," shouted Wayne to Dave who was outside at the stop tap. I grabbed the mop. "I am going to have to cap those," said Wayne, "I didn't see them over there."

It didn't take Wayne long to cap the pipes in the corner. The tap was mounted on a piece of wood on the wall and was looking very sophisticated, even though the sink itself was still on breeze blocks. Dave had said with a deadpan face that it was 'rustic' and we had all laughed about it.

"I don't care whether it is rustic Dave, all I know is that it is running water and that is bloody fantastic." I said. Wayne had even connected the waste water pipe although it wasn't connected to outside, the dreaded slop bucket was now in the annexe rather than under the sink.

"We should be in business now," declared Wayne confidently, "turn the water on Dave," he shouted to his father in law. Water started to splutter out of the tap.

"Hooray," I said and then the water pressure blew the caps of the pipes in the corner.

"Bleedin 'ell," said Wayne, "Turn the water off Dave," he shouted, "the bloody pressure is too high."

I grabbed the mop again and Dave came in from outside. "The trouble is the water pressure is very high," said Dave. I have never seen such high pressure, it must be fifteen bars."

It figured, as the water did come out of the stop tap with ferocity.

"Is it because we are in the valley?" I asked Dave

"It is often because there is a farm nearby. They put the pressure higher for farms because of the amount of water they use."

"Oh, that explains it," I replied as there was a farm not far away, just near the end of the lane.

"We are going to have to fit a pressure regulator," said Wayne. "If we go now, we will be able to get one before they shut and we can come back in the morning and fit it."

I looked at 'A'. "How much will one of those cost?" said 'A'.

Wayne went and got his trade catalogue out of the van and thumbed through it. "125 Euros," he said and showed 'A' the page.

"Yep, that's okay," he said to Wayne, "we haven't got a lot of choice." I looked at Wayne and then at 'A'. Knowing 'A''s tight-fisted nature this was just the sort of thing that might push him over the edge.

"Great, thanks," and then I added, "Now you will come back tomorrow Wayne, won't you? Because otherwise we have no water supply and if you don't come back and finish I shall hunt you down like a dog and kill you."

Wayne gave a little nervous laugh and said, "Don't worry we will be back tomorrow."

I fully expected 'A' to have a rant when they had gone, but he didn't. "It's a good job we got plumbers in to connect the water Joanne. We wouldn't have managed it with that pressure. We wouldn't have even have known what the problem was. We would have been right in the shit." I had to agree with him and although I had originally thought that 300 Euros for connecting the water was steep, I now felt that they were losing out on the job, given the amount of time they had spent on it.

Chapter 21

We awoke early the next morning as we often did. It was 3am and I made us a drink. The spate of wet weather had made the house cold. We had taken hot water bottles to bed with us the night before to keep warm and I wore a cardigan in bed. It was shocking for the end of May.

We sat talking in bed. 'A' was not as depressed as he had first been, but he still was not as upbeat about the whole venture as I was. The problem with the back boiler would not go away, but 'A' steadfastly clung to his original idea. He wanted the hot water cylinder placed above the French doors mounted on the wall. Wayne had said that it would be easier and better if it was in the main bedroom, something I had thought myself as it was directly above the log burner. 'A' thought this was inelegant and didn't want it there. We were at an impasse.

"We are just going to have to find someone to fit the back boiler. I am getting sick of this, everything seems to go wrong. The fiasco with the water is the latest problem. I hope they come back today and sort it out." He said.

I tried to allay his fears, "I am sure they will be here. I threatened Wayne yesterday and told him that I would hunt him down like a dog and kill him if he didn't and I wasn't joking. Any way they haven't been paid yet. They will be here this morning."

Just before 9am the van pulled up outside with Wayne and Dave in it. Dave was busy outside fitting the water pressure regulator and I took the opportunity to talk to Wayne about the back boiler problem.

"Look Wayne I am sorry about 'A' getting annoyed yesterday, he has got really down about this place and has even contemplated jacking it all in and selling it."

"Oh he shouldn't do that, it is lovely here," replied Wayne.

"I know; that is what I think. But listen Wayne, I want to ask you something. If you could manage to fit the back boiler, how much do you reckon it would be with all the plumbing and pipes etc?"

"You are looking at just over two grand as a rough estimate, but Joanne it isn't safe. There is nothing to stop that water cylinder from overheating and if it does that it could blow. I certainly wouldn't want my wife or kids in a house with an unpressurised cylinder, it is too dangerous."

"Oh I see," I said. "Right then, how much would it cost to have a water heater fitted, you know, like the ones the French use? I am asking for myself because 'A' is adamant he wants a back boiler but I might be able to persuade him otherwise."

"It would cost about 800 Euros."

I thought that this was a better solution. Okay it meant that the wood burner would have to be replaced with one that just provided heat not water, but we could sell the other on EBay to recoup some of the money. After all it hadn't been used, and then we would comply with French regulations meaning that if he did decide to sell the house then it wouldn't be a problem. But I kept this knowledge to myself for now.

Within half an hour of their arrival there was running water in the kitchen. 'A' who had been hiding in the bedroom came downstairs and paid them.

"Isn't that something special?" 'A' said and looked at the tap.

"Well I have to say that it is. It certainly makes life easier." I replied. For the first time in three hundred years, *Le Ster* had running water.

I usually bought my tobacco from the *tabac* in *Cleden* called *Chez Seb*. 'A' didn't go in there. But the young man who ran it was pleasant enough, and despite my pigeon French he seemed to understand me very well. He probably thought that I was some eccentric English woman who drove a van, and came in wearing her pink willies, a beret and rolled her own cigarettes. I was obviously the source of much speculation in the village as it was such a sleepy little place. That week I had noticed a poster in the window advertising a Chateau at *Trevarez* and I had mentioned it to 'A'.

'A' suggested that we go and visit the Chateau on Wednesday. I tried to object saying that Clara would hate it and only moan, but he wasn't having any of it and insisted. I had never visited a Chateau before and I was looking forward to it.

The next day was Monday again and after shopping I joined 'A' in the *cafè* for a coffee while he checked his emails. He had received a quote from Sean the roofer.

"He wants 300 Euros for fitting the Velux window and 600 Euros for replacing the guttering."

I was stunned, "Did he say anything about the pointing on the chimney?" I asked.

"No, he has made no mention of that." Said 'A'.

"Well, I think the price for the velux is reasonable but the guttering is way over the top. He is obviously trying to make his money on that. Bizarre, because when we came back from Brico Depot last week I was looking through the catalogue in the back of the van and the guttering wasn't actually going to cost much more than 100 Euros. I know he has to solder it, but there will only be three pieces and two ends. I would have thought that it would only take him a morning to do. And why hasn't he quoted for the pointing? It doesn't make sense. I am convinced the leak on the roof is coming from there."

"So what do you think Joanne?" said 'A'.

"Well I would say yes to the velux, but tell him you can't afford the guttering right now. I know it needs doing but it is not priority as it is not ruining the fabric of the building. However, you have bought the velux and you can't complete the plaster boarding in the bathroom without having that fitted first."

"I agree," said 'A', "I will email him."

The weather brightened up and it stopped raining. I was eager to get back to the pointing. I did an hour here and there when 'A' was otherwise engaged, and he didn't need me to help with plaster boarding. I had actually become so skilled at working with the cement that I had filled up some of the holes in the walls inside downstairs, which Tony had left.

Pascal and Michelle were getting friendlier and they always stopped for a chat if I was working outside. They clearly knew who was the driving force was behind the work now being done on *Le Ster*. I was slowly clearing the vegetation from the ruins and could see that they would not need that much work on them to turn them into a wood store/shed and a garage. The stone work was largely intact and they only needed pointing, a roof and a doorway fitting, although the debris would have to be cleared out of them. There was just so much to do and so little time to do it in.

The sweet corn in the farmer's field next to the meadow opposite the house was now two feet high. It had only just begun to poke through the soil when I had arrived.

Wednesday arrived and we were going to the chateau. I sat in the back of the van. We set off and followed the sign posts for the chateau. We had gone about ten miles when there was an almighty clatter. I knew immediately what it was.

"Stop the van, the exhaust has fallen off."

And as soon as the van came to a halt I jumped out of the back doors. I knelt down and looked under the van and sure enough the exhaust was hanging off at the end nearest the back of the van. A had joined me. "I need something to tie up the exhaust," I said as I opened the back of the van and looked around frantically for something. There was nothing suitable, but I did find an old pair of workmen's gloves and then I had a brainwave. I was wearing my cagoule and it had an elastic drawstring at the bottom edge. I looked in my handbag and found my Swiss army card and extracting the scissors cut the cord off my cagoule and pulled it out.

I managed to tie up the one end of the exhaust and could see that it had previously been held on with a cable tie. I climbed back in the van. 'A' was looking at his phone. "There is a Citroen garage three kilometres away," he said, "We should go there."

"Okay," I said, "but take it easy, I don't know how long my makeshift job will hold."

We got to the garage without the exhaust dropping completely off. "I think you should go in and do the talking Joanne. It will be better coming from you." Said 'A'.

'A' had said that his French was coming along, but at that precise moment I realised that it obviously wasn't. Still, months of Duolingo for fifteen minutes a day had prepared me for this very moment. I walked into the workshop and spoke to a mechanic and he told me to go to reception.

The reception was in the showroom where there were brand new Citroens and a classic car. I waited patiently whilst the receptionist dealt with an older couple, and then I approached the woman. "*Bonjour madam*," I said, "*Nous avons un petit problem*, and then I was stumped for the word for exhaust. I looked around and pointed to the exhaust coming from the back of the new car in the showroom and then I said "fell off," and made a gesture to suggest it had come off.

"*Tombre*," said the woman. Of course *tombre* was the French verb to fall. At least I had made myself understood. I explained that we had come from *Cleden* and asked if anyone have a look at it or at the very least let us have a cable tie to hold it in place until we got back. The receptionist went and fetched the head mechanic from the showroom. He came in and shook my hand. OMG! He was gorgeous. He was about my age and going grey but he was hot as hell. How did the French manage to do it? English men my age were invariably fat, bald and not very attractive but here was evidence that it was not necessarily so. Thank God I had put some slap on that morning.

I took him out to the van and Clara and her father got out. The mechanic looked around the van and he pointed to the front tyre. I was mortified and nodded in agreement. I had told 'A' a few days earlier that I thought the tyres needed air but he had done nothing about it. Then he walked around the back of the van and looked underneath at the exhaust hanging on by my cord from my cagoule.

The mechanic got in the van and took it in the workshop and we all went inside the showroom to wait. "I feel thoroughly emasculated," said 'A'.

I laughed to myself. "Why?" I said, (knowing full well why.) But it had been his bloody idea that I did the talking. He should have grown a sack and done it himself.

"Well you jumped out of the van and sorted the exhaust and then you came in here and did all the talking."

"I wouldn't worry about it," I said.

I could see the workshop from the showroom and the head mechanic had got the van up on the ramps. "It looks positive," I said, "they are working on it. Let's just hope it doesn't cost an arm and a leg."

A little while after, the mechanic came in and explained that he had replaced the rubber brackets which should have held on the exhaust with new ones and he also added that he had pumped up the tyres. I thanked him profusely and then went to the reception desk for the bill. 52 Euros which I thought was very reasonable. And they had fixed it on the spot. That in itself was unbelievable.

We decided to give the Chateau a miss. We had had enough excitement for one day.

Chapter 22

I got annoyed with the slow rate of working from 'A' but that Friday I helped him with the plaster boarding and he actually achieved quite a lot, he had finished Clara's room and had moved into the hall way. The stash of plaster boards was slowly going down. Soon we would be able to see out of the larger window in the downstairs room. As well as helping 'A' carry the boards up the outside steps and tidy up I was now putting the insulation in place. Again he was a little anal about how precisely he wanted the insulation cut but, I did it in half the time it took him.

The weather was getting very warm. The rain and the cold spell had disappeared and now the heat had kicked in. Thankfully, it was cool in the downstairs of the house. But upstairs it was hot. The insulation and the plaster boarding kept the heat in. It didn't help that 'A' did not like having the shutter closed in the bedroom. With the house being south facing it bore the brunt of the midday sun, and the heat built up during the day. The cicadas were very loud in the meadow and when we had the upstairs windows open birds flew in and out of the house with regularity. One day I saw a huge hornet which was about two inches long. I was just grateful Clara hadn't seen that, as it would have freaked her out.

It was so hot that the washing dried in a couple of hours on the rotary clothes line that we had bought from *Gifi* (a cheap house wares shop that Tony had told me about). In the downstairs of the house the back wall was sweating. Beads of water formed on the surface of the plaster. The trouble was that behind that wall was soil that had built up over the years. It really needed removing. It would be a tedious job, as it would have to be dug out by hand and barrowed out into the meadow. 'A' thought it would need to be taken away in a skip, but I knew that it could be lost very easily in the meadow. It would need to be done before the septic tank was installed as the pipes had to run behind the house to the filtration bed that was to be situated beyond the ruins.

I went for a walk to the trash bins up the lane one evening after dinner. As I came back I stopped by the land where the filtration plant was to be sited and looked at it. There were two very large oak trees near the bank to the field behind. If I remembered rightly from the septic tank report that came with the house, there could be no trees within three metres of the filtration bed. They would have to be cut down. Oak was very good for burning and given the size of the trees there would be at least three years supply of wood there. But it would need to be stored in a woodshed, a woodshed that we didn't have.

When we had visited *Emeraud Espace* on the outskirts of *Cleden* a few days earlier I had swooned over the second hand mini tractors. *Emerauld Espace* is the French equivalent of the Countrywide stores we have in Britain and it sells lots of equipment relating to agriculture and keeping animals as well as a bit of DIY.

"I want one of those," I had said to 'A'. Later that day he had asked me whether it would help me if he bought one. The most he had done before was to buy me a wheel barrow. He was actually seriously considering it. I pointed out that the trouble at the moment was that we had nowhere to store a mini tractor. The log store and the garage needed doing before we could install the septic tank because we needed those trees to be cut down and we needed somewhere to store the logs. Which came first the chicken or the egg? This project needed a plan, a serious plan on paper and for it to be followed meticulously.

When I got back to the house I sat down and made a list of everything that needed doing as I sat in the cool of the downstairs sipping my wine. Clara and her father were in bed watching a family film but I was restless. There was so much to do here and it had to be tackled methodically. Up until now 'A' had just been doing random things, he didn't seem to have a plan at all. At the moment we lived with all the power tools in the room downstairs. All of the other tools lay on the bedroom floor in the main bedroom. It was thoroughly disorganised. In the corner of the room was the lawnmower, the strimmer, the generator and a work bench. Piles of insulation were stacked up near the back wall, and then the plaster board was stacked up against the window. 'A' had said that he couldn't store anything in the annexe as it went rusty. I seriously doubted that would happen short term if the place was tidied out but the door needed replacing. We needed a serious injection of cash. Without it we could not move forward.

Saturday morning I was up bright and early and was doing pointing outside. It was coming together nicely and I would soon have nearly finished the wall of the steps. I couldn't wait to move onto the house. The stonework was much neater on the house and not as rough as on the steps I had had a little go at a small area near the door and was really pleased with the results. It looked professional. With the heat as it was now, there was no way that anyone could work in the afternoon. It was just too hot. The sweat poured off you and it was no good for pointing as the mortar dried out too quickly. As I pointed, I thought. I couldn't face another Sunday with Clara and her father. 'A' stayed in bed all day, just coming down for his lunch and then having a nap on the afternoon; it was like living with a geriatric. Clara was bored shitless. Then I came up with a plan. We could go to the beach tomorrow, and I could cook a roast chicken when we got back

It was a very hot day again. Downstairs was okay but upstairs it was unbearable. I didn't know how we were going to sleep in this heat. Unlike ten days ago when it had been so cold that I had worn pyjamas and a cardigan to bed, now it was so hot it was stifling, and I was just clothed in a pair of knickers and a vest top and it was intolerable. We lay there in the dark trying to sleep. It must have been 30 degrees. We opened the French doors at the top of the stone steps and eventually we drifted off to sleep.

'A' was in a foul mood the next morning. He didn't like the heat. I made a picnic and we set off. 'A' had an inflatable kayak and he was looking forward to taking it out on the sea.

We had decided to go westwards to *Douarnenez*. When we arrived there and made our way through the town we found it that it was nothing more than a fishing port complete with fish market that was closed as it was Sunday. There were restaurants and bars lining the harbour. We got back in the van and went out of town in search of a cove which we had spotted on the Michelin map. When we arrived we found that there was parking right next to the beach, and the usual bars and sandwich shops. We found a spot on the sand of the little bay.

It was beautiful day and the sky was blue with wispy clouds. We stayed for a couple of hours which was just about as much as 'A' could cope with and then we went and had a beer and went home. I noticed that yet again there were showers near the beach.

The next day was the usual Monday ritual and I joined 'A' in the coffee shop as he checked his emails. He had been waiting on a visa for a job in Saudi, and now it looked as though he was going to have to go back to Britain to sort it out. My heart sank. I was really enjoying my little sojourn in France and I had so much more work I wanted to do. I had originally thought that we would be there until the end of August, which would give us four months of working but, now it looked as though we would only have another month. I was disappointed to say the least but he needed work and he needed the cash. We looked at the Ferry prices.

We only managed an hour's work that day and 'A' had had enough. "It is too bloody hot Joanne."

I liked the heat, but despite this, even I was feeling it upstairs in the house. I was covered in mosquito bites and they were itching like mad. "I agree. I think now that the hot weather has kicked in we have to accept that we can only do work in the morning before lunch. It is far too hot in the afternoon."

The next morning I continued with the pointing as soon as I got back from taking Clara to school. 'A' carried on with making the door frame to Clara's room upstairs.

After an hour he came downstairs for a cup of coffee and came outside to admire my pointing. "You are getting really good at that," he said.

"Thanks, I need some more sand," I replied. I had nearly finished the wall below the steps, and when it had been raining I had done a little pointing on the house near the door where it was sheltered from the weather. I was immensely proud of that, because the stonework on the house was finer than that on the steps and it looked wonderful. I could just imagine when the whole house had been done. It would be super.

"I think I might have a go at pointing," said 'A'.

"It is very therapeutic," I said. And it was. It was peaceful and not strenuous.

Of course I had laid down the gauntlet even if it had been unintentional, and after we had eaten a French lunch of baguette and cheese 'A' said he would 'have a go' at pointing. I rolled my eyes to myself out of sight of 'A'. Nothing good would come of this. It was 30 degrees out there and the sun was baking the front of the house. The cicadas were in full song chirping away in the undergrowth as though they were laughing at his ridiculous idea to work in this heat.

'A' went out and set about mixing the mortar and was soon at it. He was sweltering in the afternoon sun and soon enough Pascal came down the lane on his bicycle.

"'A'!" he said in an abrupt manner. "It is ze wrong time of day to be doing zis. It iz too hot!"

I had to agree with him,

but I held my tongue and said nothing and stayed in the shade of the house. I was not going to be drawn into this conversation. 'A' was defiant, but I knew he would be. I had shamed him with the locals and he wanted to prove to them that he could do it. But he had gone about it in all the wrong way, starting after lunch. I tutted to myself as I listened to the dialogue between 'A' and his neighbour. Finally, Pascal knew when to call it a day and rode off up the lane to the recycle bin, but not before he had provoked 'A'. It hadn't gone long and 'A' came into the house and he was fuming. His face was bright red from sunburn, and the sweat was dripping from his brow. "Did you hear what he said Joanne?"

"I did," I replied.

"He has really wound me up," he continued. He looked as though he could blow at any moment.

I had to try and diffuse the situation. "Do you want a drink 'A'? You look very hot."

"What is his problem? Why does he have to come and comment on everything I do? Why does he have to be such a know it all? He has really pissed me off. I have been patient with him, you know. I have bit my tongue more times than I care to remember and I have been nice to him, but my patience is running out. I nearly blew out there and gave him a piece of my mind on his nosy interfering ways."

I sympathised but I could see Pascal's point of view too. Pascal and Michelle had been very helpful and supportive of 'A' when he first came, but 'A' didn't help himself. He spent many days in bed with the shutters closed fast and very little work had been done. Five years had gone by and outwardly at least the house and land appeared to have deteriorated. 'A' also didn't explain that the reason he hadn't been to France for ages was that he had no money. They would of course assume that he was just not bothered.

"Look I know he is annoying. I think he is bored shitless. I think he hangs about outside in the garden so as not to get under Michelle's feet, and he watches us. We are the biggest form of entertainment around here, you do know that. You should put yourself in Pascal's shoes. He is thoroughly emasculated. He no longer works and it is quite obvious that Michelle bosses him about. The only vestige of masculinity he has left is coming over here and giving you his 'advice'. You take it too much to heart. But he was partly right. It is too hot to point. In fact it is too hot to work at all. The mortar will go off very quickly in this heat. I wouldn't work out there in this heat and you know how much I like the sun. It is no good for you."

I feared that what I had said would push him over the edge but I had felt compelled to say it all the same. "You are right, as usual. It is too hot to work out there." I nearly fainted with his admission. Did I just hear him say that I was right?

"I will just go and brush off your pointing before it dries," I said. "You stay inside in the cool."

I went outside into the searing heat and picked up the hand brush. I turned to look at the pointing. It wasn't good. He had got the mortar all over the stonework. I just hoped it hadn't gone off yet and I started brushing at the stones. It was no good. It had stuck like shit to a blanket. I got some water and wet the brush and it appeared to be coming off but as soon as it dried I could see that it had not. In short it was a bloody mess. I sighed as I stood looking at it.

'A' appeared at the doorway. "How is it?" he asked when he saw my face. I tried to change my expression to one of pleasure.

"It's good," I lied.

He came out and turned to look at the wall. Silence followed and then he spoke. "It's shit," he said. "From now on I am leaving the pointing to you. You are better at it than me."

I was secretly pleased at this comment, but I didn't let it show and I had to put up some kind of objection to his admission. "You haven't done a bad job it is just that it is hot, that's all."

"You are being too kind Joanne. It is shit. Will that come off?" he said pointing to the mortar that had left a thin veil of white over the stonework.

"I would think when we have a good downpour it should clean it, otherwise we will have to get some brick cleaner on it."

Chapter 23

When Clara came home from school she had a letter and a book of raffle tickets. 'A' translated the letter whilst I prepared dinner.

"The school is holding a summer fair. Well I think that what it amounts to. It is called a Karmasse here in France apparently." said 'A', as I chopped onions.

"Ah, that explains the raffle tickets," I replied. "France is not so different to England. I don't know who they think we are going to sell them too as we don't know anyone apart from Pascal and Michelle. The teacher did say that we didn't have to sell any, we could just return them."

A pulled the cork from a bottle of wine and poured two glasses and handed one to me. "We will have to buy some." He said. "They are only a euro each. We will have ten."

I was amazed. For someone who was the epitome of miserliness he was going to buy ten raffle tickets, a whole book. I stirred the pan and sipped my wine.

"The prizes look quite good," he continued. "The first prize is a two hundred euro voucher for *Emeraud Espace*. If we win that it could be a deposit on a mini tractor. I know how much you want one."

I laughed. "I never win a bloody thing," I said. "In any case we have nowhere to keep a mini tractor at the moment. We couldn't leave it outside when we are not here it would only go rusty and deteriorate." But I was secretly pleased that he was considering a mini tractor to be a serious proposition. Before we could have a mini tractor the two ruins would have to be renovated. I had plans for the one to be a tool shed and the other to be a garage. They were both built higher than the road by about eighteen inches. It wouldn't cost a lot; it was more time in terms of manual labour. But I had not mentioned this to 'A'. It would have been too much for him, when he already felt overwhelmed by the amount of work still to do on the house. If only we were staying to the end of August, that was nearly another two whole months where I could do work. Still, I put this thought to the back of my head and contended myself with doing what I could before we had to leave.

A started to fill out the stubs in the raffle book, "I have put your name on five and my name on the other five," he said.

"Well that has given it the kiss of death. I never win a thing." I laughed. "Of course we will have to attend the Karmasse," I continued.

"I don't want to go." He replied. I didn't ask why, I knew. For some bizarre reason he did not want to mix with the locals. I prepared the salad and thought about it. Part of it was fear, I had realised. 'A' was not comfortable speaking French and he was afraid to make a tit of himself. I had no such qualms and indeed I didn't feel that the locals mocked me for it, on the contrary they seemed to appreciate the fact that I had a go and I apologised for my French. Then there was the fact that he was ashamed. Ashamed of the house and the fact he had done very little work in the last five years. It was nothing more that foolish pride.

"Well I had better go and take Clara. After all she is attending the local school. I have to make an effort for her sake to integrate with the locals."

The next day was Wednesday again and Clara was off school. We had decided to have a trip to Brico Depot again in *Morlaix*. A needed more insulation and he had decided after perusing my list of jobs that needed doing that he needed to buy wood to make some new shutters. Although the house was coming together nicely, it made sense to list the outstanding jobs and put them in some kind of priority order. The shutters along with finishing the staircase were at the top of the list. If we were to leave France mid-July so that 'A' could pursue his visa application for his job in Saudi, then the shutters were very important. The others were falling apart.

On the previous trip to Brico Depot to get the velux window, 'A' had spied some tongue and groove wood to make the shutters. They sold it in packs and at a very reasonable price. Although you can buy readymade shutters or have them made for you, they were not cheap and the age of the building and size of the windows meant that they had to be purpose made. This would cost hundreds of Euros. By buying the wood and the hinges separately and making them yourself, you could save a small fortune. The wood came to less than one hundred Euros. I also wanted a small thin stone pointing trowel as well. I had noticed that they sold them in the catalogue I had picked up on our previous trip.

It was a drizzly day and we didn't bother going to the beach after Brico Depot. Clara moaned about having to go to yet another DIY store on one of her days off but we promised her two DVDs that night by way of consolation. We got back from *Morlaix* just after lunch. You had to be very mindful of time in France. Most of the shops shut from midday to 2pm for lunch and it had caught 'A' out a number of times. Thankfully now he seemed to be getting up when I took Clara to school instead of wasting his time listening to Radio 4 until 10am.

'A' measured up the shutters and cut the wood to size. On my advice he had purchased some Gorilla Glue from Amazon for the stairs, and he had glued and clamped them. It had been a success. Previously some of the steps had been loose and he had to keep knocking them back into place. Now they held fast. 'A' had been so impressed with the glue that he planned to use the remainder on the shutters. But there was a slight problem.

The brackets onto which the hinges of the shutters slotted were set into the concrete at the side of the windows. They were not level and this offended 'A''s sense of neatness and his search for perfection. I had tried to hack them out with a bolster and chisel but that concrete was very hard. 'A' had even bought an attachment for his hammer drill and it had had hardly made a dent in the concrete. For once he had to agree with me that although they weren't level we would have to make do with the brackets as there were and adjust the shutters accordingly. As I had pointed out to him, "this is an old and quirky house. Nothing is level and it is no use trying to make things perfect. Any way that is part of its charm." Thank goodness common sense had prevailed.

'A' glued and clamped the first shutter and laid it on his workbench. It was bowing slightly the clamps were so tight. "Put half a bag of sand on it. That will weigh it down." I suggested.

Chapter 24

The next day we cracked on with the plaster boarding. With a time frame set in place before we had to leave it galvanised 'A' into action.

"I want to finish the plaster boarding Joanne and I want to get Clara's room plastered before we leave. I think it will give me a lift if I can see at least one room finished. It is amazing how different it looks when it is plastered. It will give me an idea of what the house will look like when it is finished. Laurie the plasterer charges ten Euros a metre for plastering." He was another tradesman that I had managed to find for 'A'.

"It should only cost me a couple hundred Euros. I thought he was underestimating the amount of square metres in Clara's room. I made a mental note to measure it up when he was engaged elsewhere.

We achieved quite a lot of work that day with my help. We finished the hall and had made a start on the main bedroom. There were large expanses of wall and by the end of the day we had used up all of the large plaster boards. Finally the larger window in the room downstairs was clear and allowed more light to get into the room. So I wiped down the window frame and gave the window a good clean.

A felt pleased that we had achieved so much that day. "We have done loads today Joanne," he said as he uncorked a bottle of wine in celebration.

"Yes we have," I replied.

Finally he had got up to warp speed on the working front. How long it would last though was another matter. I was just pleased the window was free.

The next day Sean was coming to fit the Velux window. He was going to arrive about midday. He had sent 'A' an email earlier in the week to say he was coming. I was looking forward to seeing the velux window fitted, although I still remained sceptical about Sean's abilities, I just hoped my fears were unfounded and everything went smoothly.

We sat having a cup of coffee waiting for Sean.

"At least it is a fine day today and it isn't raining." I said.

"Yes, "I am glad we are going out to *Carhaix*. I hate being here when tradesmen do work."

I had hid my laptop under some coats on the bench downstairs. I felt mean about feeling so suspicious but it was too late after the event, and I didn't have the money for a new laptop. It was no good shutting the stable door after the horse has bolted. We had decided to take my car to give it a run to keep the battery charged up.

Just after midday a white van pulled up outside the house and Sean and a young man got out of the van. We went outside. After exchanging pleasantries 'A' said "I will show you where I want the window Sean."

"Oki doki," said Sean. "Do you have any ladders?"

I was horrified. This did not bode well. His van I had noticed did not have any sign writing on it whatsoever. Not even his name or telephone number. That coupled with his lack of presence on the internet suggested only one thing to me, that he was a dodgy fucker who would do a bad job and would never be found again. I had a bad feeling in the pit of my stomach.

"You won't need ladders Sean, as the soil is built up at the back of the house and you can access the roof without the need for ladders." I said.

Come on I will show you." Said 'A' and he took Sean around the back of the house. His young assistant got a chainsaw out of the back of the van.

As soon as Sean had arrived, I had noticed that he was like a cat on hot bricks. He appeared full of nervous energy and in a rush to get started, as though he didn't have a minute to lose.

"Get that chainsaw sharpened while I go and look at this will ya?" he said to his young assistant, as he disappeared around the back of the house with 'A'.

More alarm bells rang in my head. I had no idea whether it was the norm to cut a hole in the roof with a chainsaw, but it seemed a like taking a sledge hammer to crack a nut to me. My stress levels rose several degrees. If this all went horribly wrong, then I would be the one who experienced the fallout from 'A'. I hoped to God that everything went alright.

We got into the car and set off down the lane. We hadn't gone far when 'A' said, "Sorry Joanne, I have forgotten my phone. Do you mind going back so I can get it? I want to check my emails in town." I turned around and we went back to the house.

"Thank God, you have come back." said Sean. "I can't fit this window. It isn't a Velux." He was busy fiddling with the box it came in. "I have no idea how this is to be fitted and it is crap. Just come and look at this will ya?" And he pointed to the casing of the window in the box. "Look at it. I mean Jesus isn't that just the flimsiest piece of plastic you ever saw? Why didn't you get a proper Velux window?"

'A' looked perplexed and I could feel my blood beginning to boil, and then I saw the upside. At least he wasn't going to cut a hole in the roof with a chainsaw. "You could probably take it back and exchange it." He continued and then kept repeating over and over again what he had already said.

Before 'A' could say anything as he was quite clearly dumbfounded at this revelation of Sean's, I started to speak. "Oh Sean don't worry about it. You didn't state that we had to buy the brand Velux. When you said Brico Depot was the cheapest, we didn't think you meant that we had to buy the brand Velux, and this was the cheapest."

"I did," replied Sean, "I am sure I told you to get a proper Velux. I can't fit this. It will leak it is that flimsy."

I was not going to argue with him. I was happy he couldn't do it. I just wished he would get in his van and go. "Look Sean, honestly don't worry about it. We will exchange it. I quite understand."

At that he packed up the chainsaw and got into his van. "Let me know when you have another window will ya?" he shouted out of the window as he drove off up the lane leaving us standing on the steps with the 'fake' Velux window.

"What the hell do you make of that?" said 'A'.

I turned to him and said, "I think we just had a lucky escape. I have never heard such bullshit in all my life. What the fuck was up with the man? I nearly died when he got the chainsaw out of the back of the van. There is nothing wrong with that window. It is his abilities that are in question here. No, I am of the firm belief that we had a lucky escape. I mean what if he had fitted it and it had leaked? I doubt we would have ever seen or heard from him again once he had had his 300 Euros."

'A' laughed. "As usual I think you are right."

I laughed, "I know I am right. And the way he kept wittering on and on. I just wanted to say; 'get your chainsaw and just fuck off will ya?" We both started to laugh heartily.

After putting the 'fake' velux window back in the house we went into *Carhaix*. A needed some hinges for the shutters and he wanted to look in *Ty Recoup*. We were still looking for a sideboard for the kitchen and we hadn't given up hope.

We sat in the van waiting for the roller shutters to go up on *Ty Recoup* at 2pm. A throng of bargain hunters had gathered outside. We decided to get out of the van and wait with the others for the roller shutters to go up.

It was several minutes before the roller shutters finally went up and the crowd surged forward into the warehouse. I scanned the furniture eagle-eyed looking for something suitable. There was a little two-seater sofa for 14 Euros. It needed recovering but otherwise it was sound and quite elegant. I was unsure what A would make of it though. I knew he wanted a leather chesterfield. I thought they were old fashioned and uncomfortable. There were much better sofas than a Chesterfield. But for fourteen Euros it was something that would bridge a gap as it were.

Then I spied the sideboard. It was just what we were looking for. It had three cupboards and three drawers and it was plain and unadorned without any of the fancy carving so indicative of Breton furniture. It was 40 Euros. 'A' had disappeared so I continued looking. I loved the sideboard but again I wasn't sure what 'A' would think.

I was browsing through the kitchen paraphernalia when he found me. "Come and have a look at this," he said. I followed him over to where the sideboard stood. "What do you think?"

"I like it. What do you think?" I replied.

"It is just what we are looking for. Let's buy it."

So we paid for the sideboard and arranged to collect it the following afternoon.

Chapter 25

On the way into *Carhaix* I had spotted a zebra grazing by the side of the road and then a camel. These are not ordinary sights in Brittany as you may gather and I was perplexed as to what they were doing there. Then I saw a poster that made everything clear. There was a circus in town.

'A' got quite enthused and told me it was on his 'bucket list'. Well I had a good old laugh about that. All he had to say was, "that was how shit my childhood was. I never even went to a circus." So we decided that we would go. It would be something for us to do as a family on Saturday afternoon. The tickets seemed reasonable at 10 Euros each.

The next day we returned to *Carhaix* with Clara to collect the sideboard we had purchased, but *Ty Recoup* didn't open until 2pm on a Saturday so we killed time in the coffee shop at Le Clerc.

'A' was overjoyed that the wifi was back on. It had been off for the last three weeks, and he was beginning to think that they had rumbled him using Pirate Bay for downloading films and as a consequence had decided to stop the free wifi all together. I put some washing in and went over to Lidl leaving 'A' in the coffee shop.

Since I had been in France, I had been on the lookout for a woven rush shopping bag. I had bought one years ago on a trip to Paris and it had been so useful. It hadn't been and expensive purchase, but it had long since worn out through constant use. I was determined to get another one, but surprisingly I hadn't seen one. There was a little stand in Le Clerc of seasonal items including woven rush hats and shopping bags. They were all a little too fancy for me, as a lot of them were in bright colours. There were none that matched what I was looking for. However, they didn't break the bank and I decided that in the absence of finding the one that I truly wanted I would buy one of those.

I stood in the queue to pay for my shopping bag. Saturday was a busy day at Le Clerc and I stood behind a middle-aged man in the queue. I eyed his goods on the conveyor belt with some amusement. He had a chicken, a bottle of Ricard, and an electric tennis racket style fly swatter. I laughed to myself. He clearly had his afternoon mapped out. He would cook and eat his roast chicken whilst getting slowly pissed on the Ricard and swatting flies with his newly acquired zapper. To be fair, it didn't sound a bad afternoon to me. I had to admit that the flies were becoming a nuisance of late. The heat had brought them out in droves and they loved to seek refuge in the cool of the house. I would have to purchase one of those electric fly swatters myself. The fly situation was becoming impossible. They seemed especially to like 'A' and would frequently land on him on an evening when he was sitting in bed. I didn't say, but I was sure this was because he didn't have a daily wash unlike me.

I wasn't that bothered with the flies, it was the mosquitoes that pissed me off. It didn't help that 'A' refused to shut the bedroom shutters. It was the enormous amount of vegetation outside. When I finally managed to turn the opposite meadow into a lawn and the vegetation around the house was cleared I felt there would be far fewer insects. Until then we had to do the best we could under the circumstances.

"I would like a bottle of *Crème de Mure* Joanne," said 'A' as I went back over to the table where he and Clara were seated, "and I know they don't sell it here. We will have to go over to Intermarche on the other side of town."

"Okay. I wouldn't mind a look around Intermarche and we have some time to kill before *Ty Recoup* opens." I replied.

As soon as I walked into Intermarche, I saw them. The original French shopping bags I had been seeking with leather handles. Just bloody typical I thought. Despite having only just purchased a substitute less than an hour earlier, I decided that I would buy one. I would have two. 'A' laughed. "Well I have to say Joanne, you are going to bring a certain stylishness to our weekly shop," as I placed his bottle of *Crème de Mure* in my newly purchased shopper.

We collected the sideboard from *Ty Recoup* and took it home before going to the circus. It did just fit in the back of the van but the doors wouldn't shut, so we had to secure it with some washing line 'A' had found in the wardrobe upstairs. I was wedged in the space remaining in the back of the van. I told 'A' to take any corners gently on the way home and to not 'throw' the van about as he usually did for fear of getting squashed

"I am really looking forward to the Circus," said 'A', "What about you Clara?" 'A' was having a good time, I concluded. I had been here just over a month and his mood had improved no end. We had pushed on with the house and had managed to achieve quite a lot in the previous five weeks, even though we had only been working a three day week.

When we got to the circus there weren't many people waiting. They hadn't opened the ticket office yet and we could see the animal trailers. I could see some lions, well lionesses to be precise. "Look," I said, "there are some lions over there." They were lying in the sun in their cage.

Finally they opened the box office and 'A' paid for the tickets and we went through to the big top. It was not a huge tent, but then there weren't that many people there. About fifty I estimated. We found ourselves seats midway up the tiered bench seating. There was a cage erected around the ring and a caged tunnel leading from outside to the ring.

"I am really looking forward to this," said 'A'. "That must be for the lions," he said gesturing to the tunnel.

"I do hope they have been fed," I said. Death by escaped lion at a circus was not the end I envisaged for myself, however I consoled myself with the fact that there was more meat on 'A' than myself and Clara and hopefully he would be gallant enough to try and fend them off should the need arise.

The tent smelled of animal dung, popcorn and candy floss, which was quite a curious mixture. I noticed that the ladies from the box office were now manning a small makeshift stall in the tent selling cans of pop, popcorn and candy floss that they were making on a machine.

The music finally started and they shut the tent door. A dashing dark-haired, olive-skinned man in his mid thirties stepped into the ring and the lions came prowling down the tunnel to the caged ring. The lion act was brilliant apart from the fact that I was too busy trying to take photos at the request of Clara.

"He is braver than I," said 'A'.

"Me too," I replied. I was so occupied with taking the photos that I failed to notice the hairy moment when one of the lionesses pinned the bloke to the side of the cage.

"I thought he was a gonna then," said 'A'.

The rest of the acts were good. A young woman in a skimpy outfit doing some aerial acrobatics on a large hoop, a clown, more acrobatics from the lion tamer with some precariously arranged chairs, ponies doing tricks, lamas, camels and more juggling with flaming batons from the lion tamer. It would appear that he was the main act.

"The circus would fold if he got eaten by the lions," I remarked, "He seems to be their star attraction."

All in all it was good entertainment for 10 Euros each. "I don't think they allow animal acts anymore in Circuses in the UK." I commented. "You know how we Brits are so concerned for animal welfare, but I personally think that he must treat his animals okay otherwise those lions would have him for sure." I felt sorry for them that they hadn't drawn more of a crowd for a late Saturday afternoon. "It must be hard for them to make a living at this," I commented. After all there were the animals to be fed and cared for, people to feed, numerous trucks that would need diesel.

"Well I am glad I have seen a Circus in France then Joanne, because half of the fun is waiting to see if the lion tamer is attacked," said A. Sometimes he has a sick sense of humour.

We got back to *Le Ster* and cracked open the wine and stood admiring the sideboard. It was just perfect. One drawer could hold cutlery, one could hold tea towels and the other could store tea lights, batteries and other odds and sods you needed in a kitchen. 'A' went over and opened the cupboard doors. The last one wouldn't open, it was locked and we didn't have a key.

"That is why it was only fifty Euros. How are we going to get into that cupboard? This is just typical of everything I do, one step forward and two steps back." He said.

I couldn't believe my ears. He was going into a downward spiral yet again, over something as trivial as a locked cupboard.

"Don't let a little thing like that get you down. It will be easy to fix I will have a look at it in the morning when I am fresh. I bet you could simply chisel that lock off from the inside."

'A' had clearly got the blinkers on. "And how do you propose we get inside the cupboard?" he said tersely.

"If you take out the drawer above you can get in that way although it is a tight squeeze."

I had hoped by offering a solution to the problem that it would appease him, instead he seemed hell bent on going into a downward spiral. "And then there is the fiasco with the velux window. I had a look today and I can't find the receipt, without that we have no chance of exchanging it."

I didn't see that the 'fake' velux window was a problem and I told him so as we sat chatting early the next morning in bed over a cup of tea.

"The thing is, I don't think that there is anything wrong with that window. I think the problem lies with Sean and his abilities or lack of them. I think he knows how to fit a proper Velux window and he had planned on it being a quick job. When he saw that he was going to have to read the instructions on how to fit this window, he decided that he hadn't quoted enough money for the job. Remember, he had a mate with him; a mate who he would have to pay. Those windows carry an eight year guarantee. They wouldn't give a guarantee if they were a load of old rubbish and neither would they continue to sell them if people kept complaining about them. We just need to find someone else to fit the window, and someone who will point the chimney. Despite saying he would sort it Sean never did quote for that."

He seemed satisfied with my take on the window, and didn't offer an objection. Yes it was irritating that it took an eternity to get anyone around to the house to quote for a job, let alone get them to actually turn up and do the work. Not only that, time was not on our side. The clock was ticking away and we would have to leave in three weeks.

I loved it at *Le Ster*. My enthusiasm hadn't waned since I had arrived, quite the contrary I was more enthusiastic than ever about the house the land and living in France. Admittedly it wouldn't always be summer, it would be cold and wet in the winter, but I could imagine that too. Once the house was finished and the wood burner up and running it would be very warm and cosy in the house. I could spend the winter writing and work on the land in the summer. I could imagine going out to feed the animals when it was cold and frosty in the winter and then coming back to the house where the log burner would be crackling away, having breakfast, doing some chores and then settling down to write. I would have my desk in front of the large window downstairs looking out over the meadow. Evenings after seeing to the animals again would be spent curled up in front of the fire while the weather did its worst outside. I even went as far as imagining a Christmas at *Le Ster*.

The next day after breakfast 'A' had a wash and Clara and I went for a walk. It was a lovely summer's morning and we went quite far down the track beside the river. When we got back, 'A' had sorted out the sideboard door. He was pleased as punch with himself. He had chiselled the lock straight off. "Well done you," I said admiring the sideboard.

"I suppose you will want to paint it Joanne?" he said.

I know that like most men he preferred plain wood but I favoured the more fashionable painted look. "Well it is your house and I know you like your wood plain."

How 'A' had changed. His heart attack had changed him and he had become a negative person. It was a far cry from the young man in his late twenties who had empathy for people, a young man who had optimism. Now he was negative and defeatist in his outlook on life. It wasn't even that his heart attack had left him debilitated. It could have been a lot worse. He was still alive, something he seemed to resent. "I wish I had died," he often told me. "It would have been a good death. After the initial pain I blacked out and knew nothing about it." A large portion of his health problems were down to the fact that he was unfit and overweight. He did little physical exercise. Even carrying the plaster boards up the stairs with me left him short of breath. Instead of taking his heart attack as a warning sign and changing his lifestyle, he wallowed in self pity about it and radiated negativity. Or did he use the negativity as a way of justifying his reluctance to change his lifestyle? If left to his own devices he would stay in bed all day reading, listening to radio 4 and the doom and gloom merchants and watching downloaded films and television series on his kindle. He had certainly been doing that before I had turned up and he had been there for two months before I had arrived.

I certainly wasn't going to change him, of that I was sure. When I thought back, it had been rather fantastical of him to want a self sufficiency lifestyle when he had never even grown so much as a lettuce. The orchard that we had worked so hard to plant five years ago had all but perished

Monday at the coffee shop 'A' was in a foul mood. He was clearly worried about the lack of news from the Saudi cultural bureau about his application for a visa.

"I haven't heard a thing from them and I am getting very irritated about it. They wanted me to be out in Saudi by the middle of August. They said it could take up to three months to attest all my qualifications, but the three months has passed. I don't know what to do. I have already spent the best part of £500 on employing a Notary to deal with this."

I had plenty that I wanted to say, but I held my tongue. It was best not to offer any advice when he was like this. "I don't know what to say." I said.

Chapter 26

Tuesday arrived and we had decided to visit the *Chateau Trevarez* whilst Clara was at school. I made a packed lunch and put on a summer dress for a change and I even put on a little make up, nothing much just some foundation, some bronzer, mascara and a bit of lip gloss.

The Chateau wasn't far from *Le Ster* about twenty miles away. We found it easy enough. It was high up in the hills and we parked up in the car park. We couldn't see the Chateau from the car park as it was surrounded by trees and rhododendron bushes. 'A' paid the entrance fee and the girl on the ticket booth gave us a map of the Chateau and its grounds. It was another gloriously sunny day.

The Chateau is situated high up on a hill overlooking the valley. It had been built at the turn of the century and was gothic in its architecture. Some business magnate had decided to build his dream house, but tragically two years after it had been finished, he had died. His daughter had lived there for a while with her husband and then during the Second World War it had been taken over by the Germans and used as a base for senior army officials. The British had found this out and had bombed it. It had remained derelict for many years after the war and it was only in the mid seventies that the French Government had bought it and had decided to restore the Chateau.

We visited the stable block first which was like a very large house in itself. They were beautiful and the horses must have been kept in a grand style, much like their owners and their guests. There were weird metal sculptures everywhere, apparently done by some French artist. He had used large metal pipes and had made them look like tree trunks.

"I don't think much of those," said 'A', whose taste in art is rather conservative. I had to agree with him, having similar tastes to his, but I could appreciate the skill that had gone into making them.

"They are okay and I can see the work that has gone into making them, but I don't think they fit in with the Chateau to be honest. I can only presume that they were placed here to add an additional attraction for visitors."

We walked along a wooded path which led to below the Chateau. Large hydrangea bushes dotted the hillside and framed the path that we were walking on. They were all different colours. Some blue, some pink, and some in-between with the odd white one here and there. It was a beautiful summer's day and the sky was as blue as could be with white billowing clouds sailing across it, just like in a Monet painting. In the field below the chateau stood a chapel.

"Somewhere out there in the valley is *Le Ster*," I said as we walked.

"It is beautiful here," said 'A'.

The Chateau loomed over us on the side of the hill. It was quite steep and there was a little path that wound its way up to the terrace at the side of the Chateau and we decided to take it.

The Chateau itself was not what you would describe as beautiful. It had been built out of red brick and although it had the classic fairytale turrets and beautiful windows in the roof, it had an air of melancholy about it which somewhat detracted from its beauty. I didn't envy the builders who had built it. The hill was so steep that working on the scaffolding that would have been erected to build it would have required nerves of steel. And there was something rather ostentatious about the way it had been sited on the hillside, looking down on the valley, as if much to say, 'we are better than you lot down there' it was the architectural equivalent of looking down your nose at someone.

It would be a bleak place in the winter I thought to myself. Its situation on the side of the hill meant that it would bear the brunt of storms and wind and I could imagine being in the chateau when it was howling and blowing a gale outside.

After a steady climb up the hill we walked around to the front of the Chateau where a little formal garden was laid out behind the gravel driveway. We made our way over to a bench and decided to eat our lunch looking at the facade of the house.

'A' was quite enjoying himself which surprised me. "Well, I have to say, that I am enjoying this. And, it is far better value than the same stuff in England. When I think of how much we paid for us to get into the Lost Gardens of Heligan compared to the entry price here." I had to agree that this was indeed much better value, as it had been nearly a third of the price. And it was quiet. There was hardly anyone there.

We decided to go into the house after lunch. The interior of the house still had evidence of the grandeur that once was. There was some very ornate painted panelling in the downstairs sitting room to the left side of the Chateau. It was this part that had been bombed and in their renovation the French had decided to repair the roof but leave the hole in the two floors above where the bomb had dropped. It was quite chilling to see the devastation caused by war. This was once someone's home I thought to myself, as I looked out of the windows down across the valley. The view was spectacular but in a detached sort of way. It was too vast to be pleasant, not like the view across the meadow from *Le Ster* which was comforting. It was like standing on a hill top and to a certain degree although you were inside the Chateau, it had that air of exposure to it. This was not a home I decided, it had been built with one purpose in mind; to show off. To showcase the wealth and perhaps that is why the daughter of the man who had built it had never come back to it after the war. Perhaps she felt the same way about it, I doubted from what I had read in the guide book that she couldn't afford to have had it repaired, as she seemed to have inherited a vast wealth.

The rest of the house was as impressive, but in a cold detached way. It lacked that human element in it, but it had been restored for the most part to its former glory. It even had upstairs bathrooms with large sunken baths built into the floor. It had the usual gift shop on the ground floor and much like any National Trust property back home the prices of the goods on sale were not cheap.

After the house we walked through the gardens. We visited the little wooded area with little waterfalls and we passed by the formal pool complete with bronze sculptures of lobsters sitting either side of the pool. Obviously a reference to the extravagant lifestyle its creator indulged in when entertaining guests, as these were original and not from the contemporary artist's exhibition.

The final part of our visit was to the walled vegetable garden. And that was just the best for me. Although no vegetables grew there now only wild grasses and flowers I could imagine it when it had provided fruit and vegetables for the Chateau's inhabitants. A lean-to glass house ran the entire length of the southernmost wall. Over a hundred years on and it was still standing. I read the little plaque by the greenhouse. They were going to start a project run by students to start growing vegetables that would be used in the restaurant. I was pleased to see that they were going to use the walled garden again for its original purpose.

There was a little *cafè* by the stable block and it had got quite hot now, so we decided to have an ice cream.

"I am glad we came without Clara," said 'A'. So was I, as she would have positively hated it.

(N.B – there is a website for the Chateau where you can find more details and photos – search Domaine Trevarez and I have put a gallery of photos on my website if you are interested www.joannehomer.com)

It was Wednesday again and Clara was off school. A was going to work on the shutters. I decided to take Clara into *Carhaix* that morning as she wanted to get something to wear on Saturday at the *Karmasse* and I was going to get something to wage war on the flies, as they were pissing me off no end. I had spent an hour after dinner the evening before chasing them around the downstairs of the house with a rolled up magazine, picking them off one by one when they had landed on a suitable surface.

Clara and I looked forward to going shopping without 'A'. Le Clerc had opened a new home store the other side of the road from the main supermarket and it looked interesting. 'A' wouldn't have wanted to hang about whilst Clara chose some clothes. We had decided to go to Bon Prix. The clothes were reasonably priced and it was a little like Primark, only the store was more appealing.

There was a sale on and I rifled through the sales racks. I found a sweet little mini skirt and a couple of summer dresses, and I also got her a t-shirt and a pair of sunglasses. All in all, it wasn't bad for twenty Euros.

Then it was in to Gifi, which was conveniently located next door, for fly killing equipment. I purchased an electric tennis racket shaped fly swatter, and studied carefully the other items on display. I was rather dubious about the effectiveness of citronella. Was it just to keep mosquitoes away? I decided against it in the end, as it was rather pricey and as I was unsure of its effectiveness. I concluded that it was not worth the investment. .

Then we went to Le Clerc home store. It was lovely and swish inside. You have to hand it to the French, they like their shopping. I took in everything. There were white goods on sale, and I compared the prices with the UK as I had read (a few years ago) that electrical goods were more expensive in France. However this was not the case. They seemed about the same price as back home.

The kitchen ware section blew my mind. It was just fantastic. All manner of implements and quality saucepans and frying pans, but they were not cheap, as good kitchenware isn't. I settled for a plastic cutlery tray to fit inside of the top drawer in the sideboard at 1.99 Euros. The sideboard had proved to be a very sound purchase. Not only did it provide ample storage for food and kitchen equipment, it also provided ample work surface on which to prepare food. It would look super, once I had sanded and painted it and oiled the top with Danish oil. I would replace the silly ornate brass handles with proper knobs to make it look like a kitchen cupboard rather than the sideboard that it was.

There was another reason I wanted to paint it. If we were to make a freestanding kitchen out of cupboards and the like, then they needed some kind of cohesion to make them appear like a kitchen, and not just an assortment of second hand shit. By giving them all the same treatment it would give them that sense of collectiveness. But now was not the time for this. Those steps had to be repaired and pointed before I left for England. There was only just over two more weeks before the ferry was booked, and one of those was after Clara had broken up for the summer holidays. There would be a limit to how much work I could do with Clara at home all day every day. With that thought resounding in my head, I decided that we ought to finish the shopping trip and get back to *Le Ster*, but not before we stopped off at Mr Bricolage for a bag of sand.

"Look what I've got," I said as I got out of the car waving the electric fly swatter and brandishing the cutlery tray.

'A' laughed. "That's great. It is the sort of touches like that, that turn a place into a home. A bloke wouldn't bother with such things as a cutlery tray, but it makes the difference between civilisation and savagery.

After lunch 'A' decided to crack on with making the shutters, despite the heat. French shutters are a curious thing when you look at them up close. The brackets go on the outside of the window opening, and the shutters close so that they are flush with the opening, leaving no possibility of a burglar getting a crow bar inside the shutters to prize them off. As the shutters close inside the window opening, there is no way that they can be lifted off at the hinges either. The final stroke of ingenuity is that they lock on the inside.

Given that 'A' had made them from scratch using tongue and groove planks and other wood as braces on the back of the shutters, he had made a very good job of them. But they needed to be cut down to fit before they could be hung in place and painted.

I helped him hang and mark the shutters for cutting. Even before they had been cut to size and painted they looked infinitely better than the old ones. "Shall I throw these old shutters on the bonfire now?" I said.

"Be my guest" he replied, "I am glad to see the back of them."

With time running out very quickly, I needed to get moving on repairing the steps. The next day when Clara was back at school and 'A' was busy trimming the shutters to size, I made a start on repairing the steps. Over time, the two corners of the steps had become worn. The mortar had eroded and they had become loose. I had thought about this for a while, and now I was ready to tackle them. I removed each of the corner stones and numbered them with builders chalk, then cleaned away what was left of the crumbling mortar. It was so eroded that it disintegrated like dust as I removed the stones and I swept them clean. It was easy to see why weeds had taken a foothold in between the stones.

I mixed some mortar and carefully put the steps back together. I was pleased with my efforts, and cordoned off the area so that no one could step on them while the mortar had chance to harden.

A needed some paint for the shutters so we went into *Carhaix* to get some. He would have really liked to buy Farrow and Ball paint, but he had tried ordering from their website in England and they wanted an arm and a leg for delivery to France, so we had decided to go with French paint. We had discussed the colour that we would like to paint the shutters, and we were both of the same minds that it shouldn't be the awful bright Breton blue that the locals loved. It was just too garish, and it didn't really seem in keeping with the age of the house. It looked okay on modern houses but even then there was something jarring about the colour. In France there are certain colours that are used throughout the regions. A bright blue in Breton, a brick red in the Basque region and a lavender colour in the south of France. We had decided on a darker blue/grey that would go nicely with the stonework on the house, and the Ardois slate that covered the steps.

We piled into the van and went into *Carhaix* and stopped off at Pont P (the serious builder's merchants) first to get more sand and went into the little showroom. There was an older English couple at the desk being served. I was embarrassed at the man's lack of French, and as a result they were taking ages to get served. It never ceases to amaze me that Brits will go and live in a foreign country and never bother to speak a word of the language. Even I, with my smattering of French would have looked up the words for what I wanted to buy, and rehearsed a little speech and probably taken a dictionary with me. In these days of I phones, there really was no excuse when even Google translate would do a rough job for you in seconds.

Finally the man gave up and it was our turn to be served. 'A' ordered five bags of sand in French and the man at the desk told him the price. My French numbers are not good but I thought he said 29 Euros. Sure enough when 'A' got his cash out, I knew I was right.

We went outside to wait for the sand to be bought out to us. "How much did you say you paid for your sand at Mr Bricolage?" Said 'A'.

"Just under three Euros a bag."

"Well I have just paid nearly six."

"I thought he said 29 Euros, but that is nearly double the price. Perhaps the bags are bigger or the sand is a finer quality. I don't know, but that seems a big price difference." I replied.

"Too right it does. I have just been ripped off." I was sympathetic. He couldn't very well say at the counter, and I would have probably done the same as him in his position in a foreign country. If I had been in England I would have said. "Oh sorry, cancel that, I can get it much cheaper elsewhere."

A man came out with a fork lift truck and loaded the van. I knew that 'A' would be smarting from just having paid well over the odds for the sand. "At least they load your van for you here. I had to struggle with that bag of sand on my own yesterday at Mr Bricolage."

We drove over to Mr Bricolage to look at the paint, but before doing so, we went outside into the yard to look at the sand. Sure enough, it was the same as the stuff we had bought at Pont P. 'A' was not happy. We then went into the outside warehouse so that 'A' could price up the cement as outside the store there had been a sign which translated said 'cement at demented prices'. The cement was indeed cheap, and then 'A' looked at the plasterboard.

"I have been ripped off on the plasterboard as well. It is much cheaper here than at Pont P, and it is the same stuff. Just fucking typical now I have nearly completed the plaster boarding." Thankfully he wasn't too pissed off about it, as we made our way back inside the showroom to look at the paint. Typical man I thought. Men think women are obsessed with shopping, but I would have compared prices at Pont P, Mr Bricolage and Brico Marche before purchasing large quantities of materials that I needed. The only reason I could think of to explain the prices being so high at Pont P, was that it was trade, and as such tradesman would have an account with them and probably receive a discount. 'A', just straight off the street, and without an account, would of course pay full list price. You live and learn.

We chose a paint colour, but couldn't find an undercoat which perplexed the hell out of us. It just didn't seem to exist in any form. It was a good half an hour of looking on the internet on his phone; before 'A' declared that the French didn't use one. They just slapped a couple of coats of the final paint over the primer. It didn't make sense to either of us, but time was running out and those shutters needed painting.

Chapter 27

The next day was Friday and I completed the repairs on the steps and finished the pointing on them, whilst 'A' painted the shutters. The mortar had been so eroded in between the stones on the steps that I had to go over it twice. In places I could push the mortar in several inches.

The house was taking shape and looking rather smart. The heat was still killing in the afternoons, but the trees shaded the front of the house until 11am, when the sun was high in the sky. If I was honest with myself I didn't want to go home. I absolutely loved it here. The only thing that I truly missed was the lack of internet. Of course, I missed my older children, but if we had the internet I could Skype or Face time them, and even have WhatsApp chats. I had done so a couple of times up in the village square sitting in the van where the mobile signal had been good. Having a good internet connection at *Le Ster* would make all the difference. But I had my books to get back to and I had been missing them.

"I have heard back from Laurie the plasterer," said 'A', pausing for a brief moment from painting. "He is coming a week on Monday. Clara will have finished school and we could go to the beach near *Douarnenez*. It is better that we are not here when they are working, as we will only get in the way. I am excited about seeing at least one room completed. The plastering will make all the difference."

There was still the problem of the leak in the roof, and although the weather was gloriously hot and dry at the moment, the rains would return at the end of summer, and that leak needed fixing. We had tried the usual route of asking the electrician if he knew anyone, and that had come to nothing. Tony had known of someone he could recommend, but he had warned that they might be a little too far from where we were based for him to come and do the job. Despite several phone calls and him promising to come around, he never had, and we had given up on him as a serious prospect. But I had another idea. I wasn't going to give up.

"I have seen a business card on the counter of the *tabac* in the village advertising a *couvreur*. I shall go in this afternoon and ask Seb to give him my business card and get in touch. Unknown to 'A', I had already tried to email him but had received no response (I later realised I had got his email address wrong).

Before I collected Clara from school that afternoon, I went into the tabac. As usual, several old men were sitting at the bar drinking and chatting. A hush fell over the room when I strode in wearing my dungarees. Seb had got used to me and my pigeon French, and was polite and courteous to me, even though he probably wanted to laugh. It must have killed him to keep a straight face. This is the gist of what I said after they had done the usual French greeting of '*Bonjour, comment ça va?*"

"This man?" I said in French, after tapping at his business card sellotaped to the counter. "Does he come in here?"

"*Oui*" Seb replied.

In my pigeon French I said, "I have a small problem. I have a leak in the roof of the house that needs fixing and I want a Velux window fitting. Could you give him my business card and ask him to visit me. I live at Le Ster." Seb didn't understand where I lived, and another older man in the bar, who had been listening intently, put Seb right on the property in question. Seb said he would and I thanked him and left.

I felt rather proud of myself as I sat in the van waiting for school to finish. I had managed to make myself understood. Although time was running out I had given it a shot. It would be interesting to see what a French tradesman would charge. In any event, I would like to give the locals some business. It was good for relations if we put some business their way.

The next day was the *Karmasse* and although I would rather have cracked open a bottle of wine and stayed at home; I had to do this for Clara and the locals. They had been very good to Clara, and me, admitting her to the school with no fuss whatsoever. The teacher had been most kind and his English had been impeccable. He had made the French children talk in English when he said goodbye to them at the end of the day, something that had made me rather embarrassed if the truth be told. Clara had enjoyed French school, mostly I suspected because of the fact she had Wednesdays off. The only barrier had been the language. Clara, like most children was embarrassed to speak French, although she was getting better and did try to communicate with *Bonjour* etc. There were only nine children in her class and they were mostly boys. There were two girls, but they had been friends for a long time and this left Clara out a little, but Clara spoke with fondness of the dinner lady who cooked the meals for them at lunchtime. "Even if I don't want to eat it," Clara told me, "the dinner lady always says please try a little." What a difference from the dinner ladies back home, who virtually forced you to clear your plate. Thanks to the culinary delights on offer at lunchtime at the school, Clara had tried an array of different foods and had a particular fondness for the crusty baguettes they served with every meal and she had developed a love of 'Rose de Lyon' a type of garlicky salami and patè.

I put on my fuchsia pink sleeveless linen dress and actually made my face up. Clara wore her new dress and sandals. It was 4pm but the sun was still fierce as we parked the car in the village square in front of the church. The swallows were making the shrill noises in the late afternoon, darting from building to building. It really was idyllic in *Cleden*.

Everyone was gathered at the school and *Monsieur Yves*, Clara's teacher was there. He and some of the boys in Clara's class had got a 'Guy' in a wheelbarrow that they had made for the bonfire that was to be lit later in the evening. It was the festival of a *Saint Hernin*. I didn't understand the significance of the bonfire and the guy, and made a note to ask someone or do some research on it. I had always thought that a 'Guy' was something indicative to the 5th of November in England, but it would appear that it was not exclusive. (N.B I did do research on it, and it turned up nothing, but I can only conclude that it is a homage to Joan of Arc, who was burnt at the stake and I daresay a lot of other saints – if you know different then please email me because I hate inaccuracies in a book).

I joined the few parents and children waiting outside of the school and said *Bonjour* to all who were there. I noted with some mirth that the old man who drove the school bus was with his wife. He didn't kiss the young mothers on the cheek today as he usually did before school, when his wife was not with him.

Despite 'A''s view of the locals I had found them to be a friendly lot. Many of the locals who had been out for a stroll by the river, had stopped for a chat when I was working outside the house. The reception teacher always drove her car down to the river after school, (me, with my romantic mind, suspected, or rather hoped that she was meeting her lover for a secret tryst) and she always waved as she drove past if we were outside. It was 'A' who was unfriendly, as he never went into the *tabac* and never spoke to the locals. He even avoided going to the *Mairies* office. I thought this was probably because he still didn't have a septic tank after five years, and didn't want to answer any questions about when he would be getting one. The locals must have thought him to be really weird. But I didn't want to have that label, eccentric maybe, but not plain weird. I wanted to be accepted in the village, because I really had long term plans for living there, with or without 'A'. Even if he didn't want to live there anymore, I did, and I would buy *Le Ster* from him, as soon as I could afford to do so.

We didn't have to wait long and a mini train came trundling down the road to the school. So this was what everyone was waiting for. It was a ride on mower, pulling three little wagons made out of oil drums. Each of them had been painted and had faces of animals and tails attached to them. The youngest children squealed with delight and climbed onto the oil drum animals. "I want to go on one," said Clara, tugging at my hand. "Darling, I think there will be plenty of time to go on that tractor, but it is the younger children who are having a ride now if you notice. None of your classmates are having a ride." We were new and this was obviously the highlight of the summer for the younger children, I didn't want to be rude, or disrespectful.

The train set off at walking pace with everyone else following behind and *Monsieur Yves* following with the straw guy in the wheelbarrow. It was only 500 yards to the little area beside the town hall and the sports ground. Stalls were laid out and there were games to play and to all intents and purposes it was just like a Summer Fair back home, except there was a bar selling alcohol.

We walked about the stalls. Clara had a go at 'hook a duck' which was just the same as at home, except to my amazement everyone won a prize. Clara came away with a bag of pencils and novelty rubbers and some little rubber bouncy balls. It only cost one euro to enter, they mustn't be making any money out of this at all, I thought to myself.

Then we went over to look at the plant stall, again just like England. It was just a shame that we didn't have a garden at the moment. Then we went to the tombola and Clara paid her euro, and the lady let her pick three raffle tickets. Much to my embarrassment, they all won and we came away with three prizes. I shook my head, and said "how embarrassing," to the woman behind the stall who didn't seem the slightest bit pissed off, but just smiled happily at us. We came away with a tea maker, a bottle of wine in an elaborate wine holder and a diamante necklace and earring set. I hurriedly put them back in the car before I was further embarrassed.

"Let's go and have a drink," I said to Clara after we had put the prizes in the boot of the car.

We walked back to the *Karmasse* and I went up to the bar. Everyone was so happy. It was clear that the little village of *Cleden* loved their annual *Kermasse*. I asked for a glass of rosé wine and a coca cola in French, and apologised for my poor linguistic skills. The old bloke behind the bar said it was okay, and that his English was much worse.

Clara got her ride on the train for the price of one euro. We walked around the fair and stopped to talk to the teachers from the school. The head teacher asked if Clara would be attending school in September. If only, I thought, as I explained that we had to go back to England because 'A' had a job abroad, and that the house was not suitable for winter habitation, but I added that we hoped to be back for good in the spring.

How I hoped that would be the case, but I knew deep down it probably wasn't going to be. Not next year. I seriously doubted the way it was shaping up, that A's job would happen, and then there was my ageing father. Living permanently in France was out of the question at the moment, and it saddened me that this was the case.

We didn't stay for the meal. You had to book it beforehand. I had missed that in the letter from the school about the *Karmasse*, as it was in French. It was a shame, as I would have liked to have mixed with the locals, especially when they had got a little intoxicated, it would have been fun, but there would be another time. So we went back to the house.

Chapter 28

Clara was going on a school trip to Oceanopolis in Brest on Monday. Unlike in England, there was no requirement to pay for the trip. It was funded totally by the school. All I had to provide was a packed lunch.

When I took Clara to school, we went earlier than necessary; half an-hour earlier. We sat in the van and Clara played on her I pad, using my phone as a hotspot. I checked my emails and did any internet browsing that I needed to do. That morning, I had an email from the French roofer. He said he could come and look at what needed doing later that day if we were in. I replied to say yes. There was also an email from another tradesperson, Sean, but not the roofer, this bloke fitted wood burners.

In the aftermath of Vic fitting the wood burner and the debacle over the back boiler, I had refused to give up on it. From what I had gathered on the internet, there were places in France that supplied the same type of log burners that 'A' had purchased, and they also fitted the back boiler to hot water cylinders. It was clear that they had managed to meet the approval of French regulations. Although the place in question was far from Brittany, (it was in the *Limousin* area of France). So, I had not given up. When I had originally emailed Vic all those months ago, I had also emailed another log-burner fitter in the area. He had eventually got back to me and said he would come and have a look, but by that time, 'A' had already accepted Vic's quote. According to his website, he was a specialist and he fitted the type of log burner that 'A' had. I had emailed him about fitting a hot water cylinder and plumbing to the stove.

I opened his email and I couldn't believe what I read in the email, it was from his wife. It said that, sorry but he did not fit stoves that he did not supply himself. It was as I had suspected. I knew that there was a lot of skill required to fit a hot water cylinder to a back boiler on a log burning stove. The pipes had to be at the right gradient and there should be no sharp angles for the water to rise. It would appear that stove fitters were making their money from supplying the goods, which they marked up at inflated prices. That was why Vic had originally wanted to supply the flue and all the other necessary bits and bobs. I was angry, because this was contrary to Sean's original email, where he said he would come and quote for the fitting of the log burning stove. At that time, he had known that 'A' had already purchased the stove. So that contradicted this email, where his wife had said that he only fitted stoves he supplied. I didn't look forward to telling 'A' this news. There was no way that we would get anyone to fit a hot water cylinder to the back boiler. We might as well scrap it or try and sell it on EBay. If it were me, I would just get an ordinary wood burning stove and have an electric hot water cylinder, like the French do. I have to state that these woodburners cost nearly £2,500 for the boiler alone, when purchased from a dealer who will fit them. That does not include the plumbing, the hot water cylinder and the flue. 'A' paid just over a grand for his, so you can see why they don't want to fit a boiler that a client has purchased from elsewhere. 'A' also at that time, had emailed someone in England who he knew was a good heating engineer. He even offered to pay for the ferry and accommodation for the duration while he plumbed it in and the hot water cylinder, but he heard nothing back from him. It was then that I knew that this was a no go.

Once back at the house, I continued working on the steps that week, and 'A' worked on the shutters. I had salvaged what I could of the Ardois slates that acted as paving on the top of the steps. A lot of it had eroded and had crumbled over time. We had looked everywhere for suitable replacements to match in with the originals, but without any success. I was just going to have to make as good a job of it as I could for now. Maybe if we had access to the internet I could source some, but for now I would have to make do with what I had. I was concerned that the lime mortar would not be strong enough, I really needed some serious adhesive, but again I would make do. If it looked okay when I finished, then I could bring some out with me the next time I came and re-do it.

Later that day the French roofer paid us a visit. His van was sign written in French, and he was punctual. He looked at what needed doing and although he could speak no English, we made ourselves understood. I had rehearsed my speech and had a dictionary handy to help if we got into trouble trying to explain. He seemed to agree with me about the pointing on the chimney being the cause of the leak and he made no complaints about the 'fake' velux window when we had shown it to him. He promised to get back to us with a quote. The only problem was that we had only just over two weeks before we left the country. I doubted that he would be able to do it in time, especially as French holiday season was nearly upon us, but I remained hopeful. At least we had sort of engaged with the locals on the house renovation front. Even if he couldn't do it now, he would be able to do it when we returned to the house at some point.

The sight of the roofers van did not go unnoticed with the curtain twitchers over at the lock-keepers cottage and although Michelle was subtler than Pascal, it was a couple of hours later that she came walking down the lane. I was outside of the house. *"Bon Soir Joanne,"* she said.

"Bon Soir Michelle," I replied.

"C'est Magnifique Joanne," and she gestured to the shutters.

"*Merci* Michelle," I said.

"*Le couleur c'est bon*," I was relieved. I had wondered whether we would offend the locals with our choice of paint for the shutters. Michelle continued, *"C'est sympathetique avec les ardoise."*

So Michelle wasn't just posturing, she really did like the colour. I was really happy. Although 'A' had little to do with Michelle and Pascal these days, and stayed inside the house when they passed by, to stop for a chat, they were becoming friendlier, no doubt due to the fact that I was cracking the whip, and getting some work done. The outside of the house had greatly improved in appearance over the last two months. It was in some ways quite an achievement to have Michelle sing her praises, as the old couple had cooled towards 'A' prior to my arrival. Whether it was because they weren't happy at his lack of work, or whether it was because 'A' had distanced them, I could not be sure, but whatever it was, it was no use alienating his closest neighbours. Undoubtedly seeing a van belonging to roofer who resided in the village at *Le Ster* was something that they would have been impressed with.

Wednesday came and Clara was off school. 'A' was putting the final coat of paint on the shutters. Clara was flapping about and he was getting annoyed. This was a recipe for disaster. It wasn't Clara's fault, she was bored. I had to do something. I could just see what would happen if I didn't occupy Clara; 'A' would make some mistake, or have some accident such as knocking over his paint tin, and he would blame Clara and all hell would break loose. He was hot and he was irritable.

I finished off the last little bit of mortar in my bucket and washed it out and left it in the sun to dry. I decided that Clara and I could walk up to *Cleden* and have a coffee and a coca cola at *Chez Seb*. After changing out of my dungarees we went outside. "We are just going to walk up to *Cleden*. I will get Clara out of your way so you can finish off the shutters in peace." I said.

"There is no need," he said tersely, but I knew there was.

"I need to check my emails and stretch my legs anyway. We won't be long." I said and with that I turned and said "Come on Clara." When he was like that, the best thing for it was to leave him alone.

We would be at least an hour and a half. It would take at least forty minutes to walk up the hill and forty minutes back, plus the time it took to have a coffee and browse the internet. That should be enough time for him to finish painting and calm down. I didn't know what the matter with him was. I hoped it was just the heat but I suspected there were other issues involved.

It was another gorgeous day. It was only ten thirty, but the sun was already high in the sky and it was getting hotter. The sky was cloudless, and as blue as a pair of sailor's trousers. That was how my paternal grandmother would have described it. A heat haze shimmered on the tarmac road as we started to climb the long hill up to the village. The fields were emerald green and birds flitted to and fro from the hedgerows.

"Why is Dad so grumpy?" asked Clara.

"I don't know darling," I replied, " he doesn't like the heat or work, but let's hope he calms down and gets out of his mood by the time we return. Let him have some time on his own. He is not used to living with other people perhaps that is it."

The hill was a long slog and nearly a mile long but it wasn't a problem for us.

We were about a third of the way up the hill and a car came up behind us and stopped. It was a middle-aged woman, and she asked if we would like a lift. I thanked the woman in French and declined, saying that we were enjoying the walk. How thoughtful and polite. "You should have accepted the lift Mom, we would get there quicker," said Clara but of course that was not the object of the exercise.

It had only taken us forty minutes to climb the hill to *Cleden* and we went inside the *tabac*. Seb must have been on holiday because there was a different bloke behind the bar. I ordered our drinks and the bartender said that he would bring our drinks out to us, but not before he eyed me up and down. We went and sat outside on the pavement. No doubt they would be whispering about us in the bar.

I looked at my phone and checked my emails, my messages and social media accounts. It was the first time I had purchased a drink here at the *tabac* and it was really rather pleasant. I could imagine myself doing this in a regular basis if I lived here permanently.

We stayed for half an hour. The coffee was relatively cheap and it had been pleasant. From where we sat on the pavement we could see straight down the road that we had come up. The *tabac* was ideally placed in the village to watch all of the comings and goings.

We walked back down the hill which was much easier than the way there, and arrived back at the house in time to make lunch. 'A' had finished painting the shutters and seemed in a better mood, but I knew that wasn't the last of it, of that I was certain. Something was niggling him but what?

Chapter 29

Sure enough the next day after I had taken Clara to school and was outside pointing, 'A' came out and started to pick a fight. I tried to keep calm and not respond, so as not to fan the flames of our argument, but it was not easy. Thankfully, in the end it worked, because just as I was about to really lose my temper I finished the mortar I was using and decided that it was probably best if I went into town and removed myself from the scene. It was the last day of school tomorrow and I needed to get the teachers gifts. When I announced my plans, much to my surprise 'A' said he would come too as he needed to check his emails. So that was what his bad mood was about, the lack of news about his job in Saudi. Thankfully, he was okay for the rest of the day but the lack of news about his job was worrying to say the least.

The next day was Friday and the last day of school as Clara and I sat in the van near the school taking full advantage of the strong mobile signal, *Monsieur Pierre Yves*, Clara's teacher came over to the van and knocked on my window. I hadn't seen him approaching from the rear of the van.

"*Bonjour*," I said as I opened the door. "We are not mad; we are using the internet, as there is no signal at home because we are down in the valley, so we come early to make use of it up here."

Monsieur Pierre Yves laughed. "Oh, I just thought it was because you were English and as such you need to be early." Even I had to laugh at that.

"I have something for you," he continued. He was holding a rather large cardboard box in his arms.

"For me?" I asked. What on earth was it? And why was he giving me something?

"Yes, for you," he said. "You have won a prize." I was completely bemused. Won a prize from what? I thought to myself. He must have seen the confused look on my face.

"You have won a prize from the raffle at the *Karmasse*." I was astounded.

"But I never win anything," I said.

"Well you have now," he said as I opened the back doors to the van.

"Well, thank you," I continued. "It must be France," I said and shrugged my shoulders.

The head mistress joined us. "And I have something for you too," and handed over the flowers for the Head Teacher and the dinner lady and gave *Monsieur Pierre Yves* a box of chocolates.

"Thank you," he said, "How very English." I handed over a couple of bags of bon bons for the children. It was the least I could do being as they had been so accommodating with Clara.

When I had said goodbye to Clara and climbed back into the van, I was overwhelmed and felt rather embarrassed. I hadn't hung around long at the *Karmasse* and of all the people in the village, I had won a prize. I wondered what it was. I drove back to *Le Ster* to open the box.

"Come and see what I have got," I shouted upstairs. "I have won a prize in the raffle."

"Well, I never," 'A' said as he came downstairs and saw the box. "What is it?"

"I haven't got the foggiest," I said as I cut open the tape to open the box. It was a *Plancha*. The leaflet inside the box said that was what it was, but we still didn't have a clue what that meant.

"That was second prize in the raffle," said 'A'. "We just missed out on the 200 Euros gift voucher for *Emeraud Espace;* always glass half empty, never half full.

"I don't care. I have never won anything in my life. I am astounded; and what is even more astonishing is that I was not present at the *Karmasse* when they drew the raffle. Think of it like this; as neither of us were present at the raffle, the villagers could have said, "Oh, it is that English woman from the house by the river, she isn't here, so we can draw that again." But they didn't. Doesn't that tell you something about the people here?"

We discovered that a *plancha* is a barbeque hot plate. You attach it to a gas bottle and it has a hot plate with burners underneath. It was a fine looking heavy duty stainless steel one, and it would clearly have not been cheap.

"I feel really bad that it is not gracing one of the villager's gardens. We don't even have a garden at the moment. But I am also chuffed that I actually won something." I said.

Clara broke up from school and it was the end of term. Three weeks before term ended in England. The French don't have half terms, but even so it was early

Monday soon came and with it so did the plasterers. Two of them turned up, Laurie and a helper.

'A' took them upstairs and showed them Clara's room and then we left them to it and went to the beach. We were going in the direction of *Douarnenez*, but this time we were looking for a little cove somewhere outside of the town, somewhere quiet.

We finally found a little beach about ten kilometres out of *Douarnenez*, and parked the van. There was a campsite half a kilometre back up the lane, and I thought how idyllic it was there. The only problem was that the beach was a 500 metre walk away from the car park, which meant we would have to carry everything down to the beach including the kayak which was not light.

I was feeling irritable. I couldn't put my finger on why I felt the way I did, but I was really not in a very good mood. 'A' had severely tried my patience over the last week and the prospect of having him and Clara full time every day for the next week was not a happy one. They wound each other up and I was in the middle

And then carrying the kayak was another layer of irritation I could do without. 'A' was like a cat on hot bricks, worrying about the plasterers. If he was that bloody worried then why did he insist of coming to the beach? It was all too much, and I just wanted a bit of peace I thought to myself as I plonked my bags down on the sand and laid out the picnic rug. Could they just manage to leave me alone for half an hour?

I surveyed the area. It was a very pretty little cove with low cliffs on either side. On the low cliff to the left hand side of the beach was a little cottage sitting about 20 metres above the sand. It was very sweet and I thought how lovely it must be to live there, even in the winter. There were only two other families on the beach and it was relatively quiet.

I watched 'A' drag the kayak down to the water's edge and then he walked off about ten metres to the right and minced into the sea. The water was obviously very cold. At least he was getting a wash of sorts. I glanced over to the kayak and I couldn't make out whether the tide was coming in or going out. But then a wave caught the kayak and washed it sideways. I glanced back at 'A'. He was quite clearly having a piss in the sea and hadn't seen the kayak being moved by the waves.

It was no good shouting him from this distance; dickhead that he was. I was just going to have to get up off my arse and go and rescue the bloody kayak, although I would have been happy to see it drift out to sea; so much for a bit of peace.

After two hours 'A' had had enough and so had I. Clara had needed sun screen applying and then she had needed drying with a towel. Then they were hungry and thirsty and I had to take Clara behind a rock for a pee. I never did get that half an hour of peace with the sun on my face that I so desperately craved. And we had to haul that bloody kayak back over the sand and carry it 500 yards up the hill to the van in the car park. I was glad to go back to the house.

When we came down the lane to the house there was no sign of the plasters van.

Oh dear God, I thought to myself. What the hell has gone wrong? Not something else. They surely couldn't have finished so soon. But when we went into the house, and much to our surprise the plasterers had indeed finished; and they had done more than expected. Not only had they plastered Clara's bedroom, but the hall as well, and it looked bloody fantastic.

"Well Joanne, I have to say that when we came down the lane and their car had gone I thought they had encountered some problem and buggered off without doing a thing."

"Those were my exact thoughts, but it is a pleasant surprise." I replied.

"I thought they were only going to do Clara's room, but they have done the hall as well. Doesn't it look great?" He said.

"Yes it does. But I am going to have to start cleaning up as they have walked plaster everywhere and I don't want it to set hard on the floor boards."

I grabbed a broom and started sweeping and then I got a mop and mopped the floorboards upstairs. They needed it. What with the residual plaster board dust and now the gobs of plaster, it was quite a mess.

Despite my tiredness, seeing the finished room had given me a little boost, and soon Clara's bedroom and the hall were sparkling clean. 'A' wanted to keep the floorboards bare, but I wanted to have them carpeted once the house was finished. There was no plasterboard between the beams downstairs and as a consequence you could hear everything upstairs when you were in the ground floor. A carpet would at least muffle some of that noise.

When I had finished cleaning up and we had arranged Clara's bedroom, 'A' cracked open the wine. "Thank you for doing the cleaning Joanne, it really looks much better. Only a woman could do such a good job of cleaning. I would have not done it so well," he said, handing me a glass of wine.

They had left a note saying they would be back in the morning. They wanted 500 Euros. At least 'A' thought it was worth every penny for a change.

The next morning when they came back to be paid, I wasted no time in picking their brains.

"While you are here gents, I would like to ask your advice." They seemed flattered that I asked for their advice and called them gents, and they were all ears. "Would you say this room has been lime plastered?" I asked them, talking about the downstairs, "because as you can see there is a lot of damp on the back wall. Now we suspect that part of this problem is because the soil has built up at the back of the house where there should have been a gap. That will have to be dug out, and that should go some way to alleviating the problem, but obviously there is no damp course and my question is, should it be lime plastered so that the walls can breathe?"

I had read much on the subject and thought that lime plaster on the old stone walls was the only correct course of action. It was alright plastering plaster board, that was a relatively simple and straightforward job for any plasterer but lime plastering was a skill on its own and not one that every plasterer knew how to do.

Laurie, who was middle-aged and clearly experienced, spoke. "I would say that this is just the rough base coat on the walls at the moment. And yes you could lime plaster it, but we tend to use a rail system these days, have you heard of it?" I had to confess that I hadn't. "Well what we do is put up some metal panelling leaving a small gap between the outside wall, and then plasterboard it and skim it with plaster. That usually solves the problem of damp."

"Oh right," I said. I couldn't get my head around this solution of Laurie's. Surely that wouldn't allow the wall to breath and where would the damp go? I had seen with my own eyes a few weeks ago, that in the extreme heat, the wall had been 'weeping' and a pool of water had formed on the tiled floor. Surely if they did the rail technique that he had just spoke of, and this happened behind it, there would be no where for it to go and it would make the plasterboard damp. I wasn't buying into this idea. Was it is easier for them than lime plastering? Because I knew that it was a labour intensive process and a special skill that few plasterers had these days.

"But you can do lime plastering Laurie?" I asked. "Oh yes we could do that if you want, but it wouldn't be any cheaper than the panelling I suggested.

"Oh, right," I commented, "Well that is food for thought. We need to dig out the back of the house first and that isn't going to happen this summer Laurie as we are off in just over a week's time." They said good bye and left.

"What did you make of what they said Joanne?" asked 'A' when he was sure that they had driven off.

"I don't know. But I wasn't keen on their solution of the panelling. All it would do is effectively seal in the damp, and it was clear to me that it would be easier for them. I doubt it is cheaper because there is a vast amount of plaster board to buy for a start off, and it would be a nightmare if all the pipe work and electric was behind it and we needed to get to them. I think lime plastering is the only solution, but I would very much like to see how the damp is once we have dug out the back of the house. That is a project for next year, not now."

After dinner we went upstairs and admired the newly plastered walls. It was indeed satisfying to see at least some part of the house near completion. Clara's bedroom looked very lovely indeed, and I could imagine a large rug on the floor and curtains at the window.

Chapter 30

Time had beaten us and it was time to leave France and *Le Ster* behind.

I can honestly say that I was more than a little sad to go home. I had only just got started on the work and although I had achieved quite a lot on the space of two months, I knew I could do so much more given more time.

I wrapped it up a few days later much to my *chagrin*. We had to go. 'A' had to go back to pursue his visa and I therefore, was no longer required. We went back a few days before him. The journey home was no different from the journey out and my car limped all the way home. Before we got on the ferry it failed to change gear once, and I had to pull up at the side of the road. We had minutes to spare and I had very little money to change my booking. I cursed as I turned off the engine and then started it back up again, and hoped and prayed it would change gear, which thankfully it did.

The poor old lady was twenty years old and I know enough to know that when a Mercedes automatic gearbox does this, then there is something wrong. There are only so many times it will re-start and re-set itself. So I vowed not to stop on the way home. No wheels on my wagon but I'm still rolling along sort of thing.

We got off the ferry at 7pm. It had been a long day and I was tired. The last thing I needed was to call the break down people. I had little money and had survived on a bottle of water and a cup of tea all day, having spent my last 17 Euros on a cuddly toy for my daughter that I had promised on the way out. (For some bizarre reason that I later discovered, paying by card at pump in France means that they freeze the maximum amount of money you could possibly have in petrol which is 99 Euros and even though I only had taken 50 Euros in petrol the other money was frozen and remained like that for two weeks. – Always pay cash or at the cashier with card) Things were not going well.

We finally pulled out of Plymouth and then at a set of traffic lights the car refused to change gear. I pulled over at a petrol station and turned the car off and started it up again with baited breath. It fired up and changed gear, thankfully, and we were soon on our way. I vowed not to stop for anything save an emergency.

We cleared Bristol on the M5 just a little after 9pm which I was thankful about as I knew the sun would be setting and I don't like driving in the dark. I was dying for a pee, but my ageing bladder held on to it.

We finally hit suburbia a little after 10.50pm and it was dark. Luckily we had hit a wave of green lights but three miles from home we encountered a red one and I stopped the car. When I pulled away, the car wouldn't shift out of second gear and we 'limped' all the way home. I say limped, because that is what it is with a Mercedes. If it doesn't change out of second gear it is called 'limp mode' i.e., just enough to get you to a garage.

I got Clara to bed and had a glass of wine. I was thankful to be home, but I also missed France.

Would I have stayed there if I could? You bet I would. I have never felt so at home in my life as in France and I just love and adore the country.

Chapter 31

That was last year, and as of writing this with Covid 19, foreign travel is a no go. Not as though I would have been able to go anyway. *Le Ster* is nestled deep in the French countryside, alone and neglected as it has been for so long. I do hope that one day I will be able to live there. Who knows?

But it is a house truly worth loving and looking after. I live in hope. And that it is all most of can do, live in hope.

I really would like to go out again and do more on the house. It needs a shed load of cash and time spending on it and 'A' did never get his visa for Saudi, so at the moment it is on the back burner. The last email I had from him, he said he wanted shut of it. I have not got the money to buy it yet, but I would if I could, I feel sorry for the house. I dearly love the place and really want to see it fully restored. I would love to meet the locals again and go up to *Chez Seb* for a coffee. Still, I might send him a copy of this book so that he can put it on his shelf and all the locals can talk about it and laugh about the eccentric English woman who rolled her own, wore pink wellies, drove a van and spoke appalling French.

If you would like to see any pictures about *Le Ster* and the places we visited, then please have a look at my website where I shall post some. If you want to know anything more, and then message me and keep an eye out on my blog because who knows, things may get better for me and I might, just might, one day live in France.

Bonne Chance with your adventures in France.

Jo x

If you liked this book then why don't you go along to my website and subscribe for your FREE EBook. You will also find a gallery of photos on my Website of the places we visited in this book and of the house itself. www.joannehomer.com

About the Author

Joanne is a woman of a 'certain age' as the French say. Slightly eccentric, she is a self-confessed Francophile and loves all things French, especially the food, wine and the men; she just can't resist that sexy accent. Joanne has a collection of berets that embarrass her youngest child, but that are so useful in the winter when she is out walking the family Labrador.

When she is not writing, Joanne has six children and five grandchildren to keep her busy. Thankfully, cooking is one of her hobbies. She also likes to 'have a go' at painting seascapes and she has a fondness for dramatic skies.

Joanne usually writes Contemporary Women's Fiction and you will find her other books on her website www.joannehomer.com.

If you enjoyed this book then please leave a review on Amazon where you purchased the book or on her Face book page. She would be so grateful.

Printed in Great Britain
by Amazon